ESPECIALLY FOR:

_____

FROM:

_____

DATE:

_____

CHOOSE
COURAGE

3-MINUTE DEVOTIONS
FOR MEN

DAVID SANFORD

BARBOUR BOOKS
An Imprint of Barbour Publishing, Inc.

ISBN 978-1-64352-410-8

Some content in this book has been abridged from previous writings by the same author.
Published by Barbour Books, an imprint of Barbour Publishing, Inc., 1810 Barbour Drive, Uhrichsville, Ohio 44683, www.barbourbooks.com

Our mission is to inspire the world with the life-changing message of the Bible.

Member of the
Evangelical Christian
Publishers Association

Printed in the United States of America.

INTRODUCTION

Congratulations! It's great that you have started reading *Choose Courage*. If a friend or family member gave this book to you, be sure to thank them when you're done reading it. Then consider reading it a second time to highlight truths you want to remember for years to come.

Each page of *Choose Courage* is designed to be read, considered, and then applied as you go to the Lord in prayer. Ideally, you'll read only one page a day. If you "cheat" and read an extra page or two, however, that's okay. But make a point of picking up this book every day. Here's the plan for each page:

- Minute 1: Read and reflect on God's Word
- Minute 2: Read real-life application and encouragement
- Minute 3: Pray and apply today

As you read, don't be surprised to find yourself becoming a man of greater backbone, boldness, determination, durability, faithfulness, fortitude, grit, guts, mettle, moxie, patience, persistence, resilience, resolution, stamina, staying power, steadfastness, straightforwardness, stick-to-it-iveness, trustworthiness, and tenacity.

Start telling friends, family, coworkers, and others what you're learning and doing that's new for you. After all, they want more courage too!

When they saw the courage of Peter and John
and realized that they were unschooled, ordinary
men, they were astonished and they took note
that these men had been with Jesus.
ACTS 4:13

MARCHING ORDERS

"Do not be afraid; do not be discouraged, for the
LORD your God will be with you wherever you go."

JOSHUA 1:9

In Joshua 1:1–9, the Lord God, gave six specific "choose courage" orders to Joshua. Because each is exemplified and reiterated by Jesus and His apostles, these commands apply equally to you and me today.

1. *Be strong*: Luke 2:40; 1 Corinthians 15:58, 16:13; Ephesians 6:10; 2 Timothy 2:1; 1 Peter 5:10.

2. *Be courageous*: Matthew 14:27; Mark 6:50; Acts 4:13; 1 Corinthians 16:13.

3. *Know God's Word*: Matthew 22:29; Luke 24:27, 24:32, 24:45; John 2:22, 7:38; Acts 8:35, 17:2, 18:28; Romans 1:2, 15:4; 1 Corinthians 15:3–4; 1 Timothy 4:13; 2 Timothy 3:15–17; 1 Peter 3:15; 2 Peter 1:20, 3:16.

4. *Obey God's commands*: Matthew 5:19, 28:20; Mark 10:19; Luke 1:6; John 15:10–17; Acts 17:30; Romans 7:12; James 1:22–25; 2 Peter 3:2; 1 John 2:3–4, 3:22–24, 5:3.

5. *Do not be afraid*: Matthew 8:26, 10:26, 14:27, 28:10; Mark 6:50; Luke 5:10, 12:4, 12:7, 12:32; John 6:20, 14:27; Acts 9:27, 18:9; Ephesians 6:19–20; Hebrews 13:6; 1 Peter 3:14; 1 John 4:18.

6. *Do not be discouraged*: Matthew 28:20; John 14:16–17; Philippians 4:9; Hebrews 13:5.

Lord, You want courageous men to obey Your commands.
Empower me to do that more and more.

WHEN LIFE ISN'T EXCITING

"In frenzied excitement it eats up the ground;
it cannot stand still when the trumpet sounds.
At the blast of the trumpet it snorts, 'Aha!'"

JOB 39:24-25

Did you know the words *excite*, *excited*, and *exciting* don't appear in most modern Bible translations? In the New International Version, the one exception is quoted above—but the Lord is talking about horses, not men!

Contrary to the not-so-subliminal messages we see on social media, our lives are not meant to be exciting every day. Most lives are normal and routine.

So when the Lord blesses us with fresh new experiences of His wonderful providence, we gladly praise Him. But we also want to praise Him every other day too. Our failure always comes with the *loss* of potential future blessings.

That's why the apostle Paul reminds us to pray every day "with thanksgiving" (Philippians 4:6) and to "give thanks in all circumstances; for this is God's will for you in Christ Jesus" (1 Thessalonians 5:18).

Every day, we can thank the Lord for who He is—for His sovereignty (greatness), providence (guidance), holiness (glory), love (graciousness), and mystery ("God alone knows").

No matter what, our greatest joy comes from praising our God.

Lord, You want courageous men to cease striving for excitement. Thank You for encouraging me to do the same.

DON'T FORGET GOD'S MIRACLES TODAY

You are the God who performs miracles;
you display your power among the peoples.
PSALM 77:14

Over the years, how many miracles has the Lord done for you?

If you're not sure, I encourage you to take a few minutes to create a list of the miracles God has done for you and your family. Remember, miracles do not have to be flashy or spectacular. They just have to be *the Lord at work*, making something happen that otherwise would not have occurred.

Perhaps the Lord has prompted someone to give you an unexpected financial gift for the exact amount you needed and prayed for, even though no one could have known about your need.

Other examples of miracles today include the Lord's providence and sovereignty to. . .

give someone the gift of faith for salvation,
make a person wholeheartedly dedicated to God,
provide someone with his first career job,
bring two people together who later marry,
heal a sick person fully and completely.

How many miracles are on your list? Remembering them will encourage and strengthen you for many years to come.

---

*Lord, You want courageous men to remember
what You have done. Remind me.*

WHAT'S IN A NAME?

Jesus looked at him and said, "You are Simon
son of John. You will be called Cephas"
(which, when translated, is Peter).

JOHN 1:42

In the Old Testament, we hear a lot about the twelve sons of Jacob (also known as Israel), including his second son, Simeon. While Simeon had tens of thousands of descendants, no one else has that name in the Old Testament.

By the time of Jesus, however, the name abounds, often in the New Testament form *Simon*. The most famous is the apostle Simon, whom Jesus calls Peter (and who, in Greek, calls himself Simeon in 2 Peter 1:1).

Others include an elderly prophet (Luke 2:25–35), a brother of Jesus (Matthew 13:55), an apostle called "the Zealot" (Luke 6:15), and the father of Judas Iscariot (John 6:71). Still others include a wealthy Pharisee (Luke 7:40–47), a wealthy leper healed by Jesus (Matthew 26:6), the man forced to help carry Jesus' cross (Luke 23:26), a sorcerer (Acts 8:9–24), a tanner (Acts 9:43), and a church leader in Antioch (Acts 13:1).

Not all of these men followed Jesus. Thankfully, most did— and some gave their lives in martyrdom rather than dishonor the name of their Lord.

---

*Lord, You want courageous men to bring
honor to Your name. I want to do just that.*

A PROFOUND TRUTH

I desire you more than anything on earth.

PSALM 73:25 NLT

In the Psalms, Gospels, and Epistles, we discover a profound truth. Can you see it in the following verses?

The psalm writer Asaph wrote, "Whom have I in heaven but you? I desire you more than anything on earth. My health may fail, and my spirit may grow weak, but God remains the strength of my heart; he is mine forever" (Psalm 73:25–26 NLT).

In the Sermon on the Mount, Jesus said, "Store up for yourselves treasures in heaven, where moths and vermin do not destroy, and where thieves do not break in and steal. For where your treasure is, there your heart will be also" (Matthew 6:20–21).

The apostle Paul admitted about his "thorn in the flesh" that "three times I pleaded with the Lord about this, that it should leave me. But he said to me, 'My grace is sufficient for you, for my power is made perfect in weakness.' Therefore I will boast all the more gladly of my weaknesses, so that the power of Christ may rest upon me" (2 Corinthians 12:8–9 ESV).

The profound truth is this: Everything we desire, want, and need is found in the Lord, and the Lord alone. Why look anywhere else?

Lord, You want courageous men to desire You.
I want and need You above all else.

LOVING GOD WITH ALL OUR MIND

"You must love the LORD your God with
all your heart, all your soul, all your mind."

MARK 12:30 NLT

Our mind can't be separated from the rest of our being. That's why it's so important to remember the following six VIPs (Very Important Principles):

1. The most important command in all of scripture begins with the verse quoted above.

2. In his day, Albert Einstein was a genius. He wrote: "Most people say that it is the intellect which makes a great scientist. They are wrong; it is the character."

3. Solomon was even wiser than Einstein, yet he blew it. "Above all else, guard your heart, for everything you do flows from it" (Proverbs 4:23).

4. If we don't love God with all our being, do we really love Him? That's why it's so important to love the Lord our God with our entire being—including our mind (Deuteronomy 6:5).

5. We need to watch out that the world doesn't warp our mind. "Do not be conformed to this world, but be transformed by the renewal of your mind" (Romans 12:2 ESV).

6. We need to get to know God's Word better and better. "But as for you, continue in. . .the Holy Scriptures, which are able to make you wise for salvation" (2 Timothy 3:14-15).

---

*Lord, You want courageous men to love You
whole-mindedly. That's my desire as well.*

EMBRACING THE GOOD NEWS!

For I am not ashamed of this Good News about
Christ. It is the power of God at work.

ROMANS 1:16 NLT

The more I read the words of Jesus, the more I'm convinced His message is "the power of God at work, saving everyone who believes" (Romans 1:16 NLT).

Only the Good News of Jesus Christ fulfills our greatest desires: to achieve significance, to love, and to be loved.

Only His Good News meets our greatest relational needs: to more fully know others, to accept others, to forgive others, to love others, and to enrich our families.

Only His Good News takes away our greatest fears: of an uncertain future, of the call of eternity, of loneliness, of failure, of guilt, and of shame.

It's an incredible feeling to know I no longer have any reason to be lonely or live in fear. The Good News is the fall of humanity reversed!

---

*Lord, You want courageous men to embrace
the Good News. I want to do that fully.*

JESUS, INFINITE AND ETERNAL

"I am in them and you are in me. May they experience
such perfect unity that the world will know that you
sent me and that you love them as much as you love me."

JOHN 17:23 NLT

During the Last Supper and immediately afterward, Jesus said some astonishing things to the disciples. His last bombshell was that God the Father loves the disciples "as much as you [Father] love me."

The things Jesus says in John 13–17 remind us of the Lord's infinite and eternal nature. We do well to meditate on both. If God the Father is infinite and eternal, can He really be half-hearted about anything? Of course not. So if He loves the disciples, He loves them as much as He loves His own dear Son.

What does that mean to you and me? That God knows us (1 Corinthians 13:12). That He is for us (Romans 8:31). That He has plenty of power and ability to help us through whatever difficulties we face—in fact, He has *all* power and ability!

---

*Lord, You want courageous men to
believe everything Jesus said. I do!*

GOD LOVES YOU!

The grace of the Lord Jesus Christ and the love of God
and the fellowship of the Holy Spirit be with you all.

2 CORINTHIANS 13:14 ESV

I often thank the Lord for His greatness and goodness, especially the extreme measures He took to forgive our sins so we can have a restored relationship with Him. That's what Christmas, Good Friday, and Easter are all about. All we have to do is acknowledge what Jesus Christ did for us, say thank you, and invite Him into our lives.

Yet it's sometimes hard to shake the feeling that God is disillusioned with us. The reality is, however, that God is crazy in love with us—no matter what we've done, and no matter what mess we're in. Best of all, His love doesn't demand any promises from us about the future. He wants to be invited into our hearts and lives, and He does the rest now and for eternity. That's good news, indeed!

---

*Lord, You want courageous men to
embrace Your love for them. Thank You!*

INVITE GOD BACK INTO YOUR LIFE

How long, LORD? Will you forget me forever? How long will
you hide your face from me? How long must I wrestle with
my thoughts and day after day have sorrow in my heart?

PSALM 13:1-2

In dark times—after the death of a close friend or loved one, a
horrible accident, acts of terrorism, natural disasters, and other
human tragedies—God can seem infinitely far away. And if we
feel that God has walked out of our lives, we might even ask,
Do I want God back?

No matter how deeply we bury grief in our souls, it doesn't
go away. In the end, God wants us to discover that He's still
there with us. . .even when we were the ones who did the
leaving in the first place.

Maybe you have been taught that it's impossible to
come back to God. You may have felt God wouldn't take
you back anyway. Not true! God's love, mercy, and grace are
unconditional.

The course of your life could change today based on a
single decision, either to consciously lock God out—or to open
the door of your heart and invite Him in.

---

*Lord, You want courageous men to say yes
to You. I'm saying yes to You right now.*

ASK GOD TO MAKE HIMSELF REAL TO YOU

Against all hope, Abraham in hope believed and so
became the father of many nations, just as it had
been said to him, "So shall your offspring be."

ROMANS 4:18

God wants us to know that He is always there with us. Sometimes that's hard to believe. After all, we can't see or touch Him.

I find that many people wish, in their heart of hearts, that they could believe that God hasn't abandoned or rejected them. Maybe you've consciously cursed God. Maybe you've only rejected the church. Maybe you've simply lacked the confidence to say, "God, if You're real, please make Yourself real to me."

God isn't afraid of our questions and struggles. (Just take a look at the book of Psalms, which is filled with questions and struggles.) As author Philip Yancey reminds us, the one mistake we dare not make is to confuse God (who is good) with *life* (which is hard).

God feels what we feel—and is taking the most radical steps possible to redeem the present situation. There is always hope.

Lord, You want courageous men to ask You to make Yourself real in their lives. Please do that in my heart and life today.

EMBRACE FAITH IN
GOD OUR CREATOR

"God did this so that they would seek him and perhaps reach
out for him and find him, though he is not far from any one
of us. 'For in him we live and move and have our being.'"

ACTS 17:27–28

We live in a very confused world, a world that's trained itself to
make two huge errors of thinking.

First, people confuse *feelings* with *reality*. A man wakes up
one morning, rolls over, sees his wife, and realizes he doesn't
have any loving feelings for her. This lack of feelings of love
shocks him so much he decides it must be the truth.

Second, people confuse an *event* with *fate*. One morning,
a man decides he doesn't love his wife anymore. Another morning, he decides he doesn't believe in the Lord God, creator of
heaven and earth. The man then acts as if there is no going
back, no possibility of changing his mind, and no chance he
made the wrong decisions.

I like to call these two huge errors of thinking "pick-and-
choose reality." What terrible confusion, grief, and sorrow
they've wrought on mankind.

Let's reject these ways of thinking and instead embrace
faith in God our Creator!

---

*Lord, You want courageous men to reject "pick-and-choose
reality" and embrace faith in You, their Creator. I do!*

LISTEN WELL

As for you, you were dead in your transgressions and sins,
in which you used to live when you followed the ways of this
world and of the ruler of the kingdom of the air, the spirit
who is now at work in those who are disobedient.

EPHESIANS 2:1–2

Our words don't always convey what we mean.

For example, if someone tells me he doesn't believe
the Bible—in fact he distrusts it and doesn't want to read it
anymore—it sounds like he hates God's Word. That may be the
case. Or he may be saying—even if he doesn't realize it—that
he's rejecting the distorted, false images of the Bible that he's
been exposed to because of an angry, domineering parent.

If a graduate student tells me she doesn't love God—in fact
she hates God and doesn't want anything to do with Him—it
sounds like she hates the God of the Bible. That may be the
case. Or she may be saying—even if she doesn't realize it—that
she's rejecting the ugly, even repulsive images of God she's
been exposed to in some university class.

Let's begin to *really* listen to what others are saying—or
aren't saying.

---

*Lord, You want courageous men to hear the meaning
behind people's words. Help me to listen well.*

BE FORGIVEN BY GOD AND FORGIVE OTHERS

For he has rescued us from the dominion of darkness
and brought us into the kingdom of the Son he loves,
in whom we have redemption, the forgiveness of sins.

COLOSSIANS 1:13-14

Forgiveness is powerful both vertically in our relationship with God and horizontally in our relationships with others.

In the Gospels, Jesus linked God's forgiveness of our sins with our forgiveness of those who have sinned against us. We see this teaching first in the Lord's Prayer (Matthew 6:9-13) and then throughout Jesus' earthly ministry.

Not surprisingly, the theme continues in the epistles. To Paul, Peter, John, and the other apostles, God's forgiveness is closely related to our forgiveness. We forgive because we know that Jesus died for our sins—and not for ours only, but for the sins of the whole world (1 John 2:2).

Such vast forgiveness shows heaven's almighty power over Satan's dark and doomed kingdom. When we gladly believe that Jesus died for all sin, and when we truly extend forgiveness to others, we demonstrate the life-changing power of the Gospel.

Lord, You want to forgive men and You want them to courageously forgive others. I now forgive _____.

PRACTICE RADICAL FORGIVENESS

"But while he was still a long way off, his father saw him and was filled with compassion for him; he ran to his son, threw his arms around him and kissed him."

LUKE 15:20

The Bible says disciplining a child is important, but what about when a child does something especially bad? In such cases, proportional discipline isn't possible. After asking for the Lord's wisdom, I find it best to practice radical forgiveness. In fact, I emphatically promised my children that I would always do so. Each of them knows that confessing especially bad behavior to me will be met with deep love and instant and full forgiveness. This is true for my children at every age, even adulthood. It's a real-life example of the prodigal story in Luke 15:11–32, which portrays the Lord's marvelous, amazing mercy and grace.

In my study of the rise of ardent disbelief, I discovered that Christian parents focusing on legalistic man-made rules (while ignoring the Lord's most important commands) ended up propelling many of their children *away from* God, the Bible, and the Church—sometimes as early as age seven or eight.

How good that the Lord repeatedly invites us to ask Him for wisdom in every sphere of life. May you and I do so regularly.

Lord, You want courageous men to practice radical forgiveness. I'm ready.

LEARN FROM OTHERS' MISTAKES

Submit to one another
out of reverence for Christ.

EPHESIANS 5:21

In every major sphere of life you'll find stories about the tragic results when someone fails to submit to God, let alone humbly yield to other trustworthy people.

One of the most tragic figures in the art world is Vincent van Gogh. He thought he could have a relationship with God while neglecting or avoiding meaningful relationships with others here on earth. He constantly rebuffed the encouragement, counsel, and advice of his older brother, Theo, and others who loved him.

Ultimately, van Gogh's despair brought him to the point of abandoning faith in God. Apparently, he never considered that God, rather than failing him, had been trying to speak to him and care for him through those who deeply loved him.

What a difference if van Gogh had only listened to them. He could have fulfilled his destiny as an artist to the glory of God. Instead, van Gogh ended his own life with a bullet.

We don't have to repeat van Gogh's mistakes. Each day we can learn what it means to submit to God and to humbly defer to the counsel of others we trust.

Lord, You want courageous men to submit to You and to others. Please give me wisdom in knowing how.

EMBRACE HUMILITY, TRUST, AND SUBMISSION

In the same way, you who are younger, submit yourselves to your elders. All of you, clothe yourselves with humility toward one another, because, "God opposes the proud but shows favor to the humble." Humble yourselves, therefore, under God's mighty hand, that he may lift you up in due time. Cast all your anxiety on him because he cares for you.

1 PETER 5:5–7

It's probably an exaggeration to say most people hate the word *submit*. But we might have mixed feelings about submission, if we think about it at all.

I believe there's nothing the devil would like better than for us to have no idea what it means to submit to God and to a small handful of highly trusted individuals who know and love us.

True submission is built on humility and trust, and neither of those qualities are natural for us. Instead, we're mostly good at trying to be self-reliant and sometimes reckless.

When we embrace humility, however, the transforming power of God's grace is released in and through our lives. If we come to others in humility, God's grace is poured out through us, making it possible to build relationships of trust.

Of course, we can't trust everybody. Then again, we can't trust nobody.

Lord, You want courageous men to be humble,
build trustworthy relationships, and submit.
Show me who those people are in my life.

REJECT THREE MISCONCEPTIONS ABOUT SUBMISSION

Have confidence in your leaders and submit to their authority, because they keep watch over you as those who must give an account. Do this so that their work will be a joy, not a burden, for that would be of no benefit to you.

HEBREWS 13:17

Let's look at what the Bible does—and doesn't—say about submission in order to clear up several misconceptions.

First, submission isn't possible unless we reject the American ideal of rugged individualism. Otherwise, we'll know nothing of submitting to others' strengths and pay a dear price.

Second, scripture doesn't give us the authority to command others to submit to us. That would be as ludicrous as commanding someone to love or respect us. Submission must be earned. It builds on the positive aspects of true humility and grace-filled trust. Only when those two things are in place is healthy, Christlike submission possible.

Third, submission doesn't mean taking orders. Instead, it means being *willing* to yield or defer to the strengths of others. This is true not only in marriage but also in every other major sphere of life, including our relationship with God.

Lord, You want courageous men to embrace biblical submission. Help me see through the misconceptions to what Your Word says.

EXERCISE WELL-PLACED, WELL-EARNED TRUST

"Submit to God and be at peace with him;
in this way prosperity will come to you."

JOB 22:21

True trust is well placed and well earned. We can't simply say, "Trust me." Trust has prerequisites.

We all have very active trust processors. When we get hurt by others, our trust meter's sensitivity goes way up. It's all too easy to trust no one, not even God. If that happens, however, we end up forfeiting good things in life.

Live in isolation long enough and, yes, you can develop phenomenal talents and skills. But in isolation you can't develop character, or integrity, or leadership skills. Those are developed only within authentic relationships built on humility, trust, and submission.

Keep in mind that submission isn't primarily about power. It's not even primarily about recognizing and following the leadership of those over us, although that's important. Instead, submission involves actively listening to and heeding the counsel of others.

Whenever we turn off and tune out what God and trusted friends have to say, we're bound to lose our way and get needlessly hurt. That's no way to live.

---

*Lord, You want courageous men to abhor
rugged individualism. I was born with that
DNA, but I choose to exercise trust instead.*

SEE THE PERFECT MODEL WITHIN THE TRINITY

May the grace of the Lord Jesus Christ, and the love of God,
and the fellowship of the Holy Spirit be with you all.

2 CORINTHIANS 13:14

We're all going to experience crises of life, usually when we least expect them, often from a completely unexpected source. Ahead of time we have a decision to make. Are we going to handle life as rugged individualists? Or are we going to turn to God in humility, trust, and submission?

Ultimately, when it comes to submission, trust, humility, or any other aspect of life and godliness, we see the perfect model within the Trinity—God the Father, God the Son, and God the Holy Spirit. Within the Trinity, there are different functional roles yet complete equality, harmony, and intimacy. We never have to worry about the Father dominating the Son, or a power struggle breaking out between the Son and the Spirit. Instead, they're One.

When we find ourselves struggling to submit to God, let's get on our knees and ask for the Holy Spirit to fill us (see Ephesians 5:18). That may sound old-fashioned; it may sound mystical, but it works. Not just for today—for a lifetime.

---

*Lord, You want courageous men to be unified with You,
much like the Trinity. Please empower me by Your Spirit.*

THE GIFT OF ENCOURAGEMENT

When he arrived and saw this evidence of God's blessing,
he was filled with joy, and he encouraged the
believers to stay true to the Lord.

ACTS 11:23 NLT

As part of a devotional application Bible project, I spent many hours creating a comprehensive list of the Bible's 121 major characters, including Barnabas, the subject of today's verse.

Because the Bible is true to life, these people are shown to have strengths and weaknesses, stellar moments and sometimes smack-your-forehead failures. We don't always want to follow their examples. Instead, we want to *heed* them.

Like Phinehas, I must be willing to stand up for what's right.

Like David, I will share my heart with God in any and every circumstance.

Like Cornelius, I will be glad God's salvation is freely offered to all people.

Unlike Eli, I will not devalue God in my heart and affections.

My favorite Bible character is Levi, nicknamed Barnabas ("Son of Encouragement"). He was a close friend of Jesus' twelve disciples, the apostle Paul, the doctor Luke, and many others. I love the fact that Luke says in Acts 11:23, Barnabas "was filled with joy."

What a gift of God to have such friends, and to *be* such a friend.

Lord, You want courageous men to encourage others.
Who do You want me to encourage today?

HOW TO PRAY FOR YOUR FAMILY

"As for me, far be it from me that I should sin against
the LORD by failing to pray for you. And I will teach
you the way that is good and right. But be sure to fear
the LORD and serve him faithfully with all your heart;
consider what great things he has done for you."

1 SAMUEL 12:23–24

When I ask other men how they came to faith, some look down
and say, "My testimony is pretty boring. I grew up in a loving
Christian family." I slap the table hard for emphasis and reply, "I
wish I had such a great testimony."

I often quip that I'm from a long line of atheists in Seattle.
When I fully dedicated my life to Jesus Christ at age thirteen,
the fallout was harsh. Then again, a decade later I married my
wife, Renée, and a year after that we started our family. Renée
and I have gladly and joyfully dedicated every child and grand-
child to the Lord.

Here is an example of how I pray: "Lord, thank You again
for my nine grandsons. May each one grow up to be a hand-
some, winsome, wise, and godly young man who loves You
wholeheartedly and loves others well."

Why not ask for everything we could want?

---

*Lord, You want courageous men to pray big prayers
for their loved ones. I'm going to do that right now.*

MORE VALUABLE THAN BIRDS

Now the LORD God had formed out of the ground all the
wild animals and all the birds in the sky. He brought them
to the man to see what he would name them; and whatever
the man called each living creature, that was its name.

GENESIS 2:19

I love listening to the birdcalls outside my windows. Their calls
fill the air 360 degrees around my house. Do I know the number of birds? No. Have I named any of them? No. Do I feed
them? No. Yet the Lord God does. And He cares enough to
know when each falls to the ground.

Yesterday, after hearing our cats jump extra hard, I quickly
rushed into our kitchen and found feathers everywhere. I got
on my knees and found the sparrow, dead yet still warm, underneath our dining room table.

As quick as I was, God already knew.

No wonder Jesus said, "Are not two sparrows sold for a
penny? Yet not one of them will fall to the ground outside your
Father's care" (Matthew 10:29).

And no wonder He said, "Look at the birds of the air; they
do not sow or reap or store away in barns, and yet your heavenly Father feeds them." Then He asks: "Are you not much
more valuable than they?" (Matthew 6:26).

---

*Lord, You want courageous men to remember their
God-given worth. Thank You for Your love and care.*

WHAT WE KNOW AND
WHAT GOD KNOWS

Do you not know? Have you not heard? The LORD
is the everlasting God, the Creator of the ends
of the earth. He will not grow tired or weary,
and his understanding no one can fathom.

ISAIAH 40:28

Scripture describes God's understanding as being beyond comprehension. There's no comparison. His knowledge is infinite and eternal. What I know isn't even 0.00001 percent of what He knows. That's true about everything I know—both what I know apart from God's Word and what I know from it. Scripture reveals important, eternal truths you and I need to know, but let's never assume that's all God knows.

We dare not forget that the Lord knows everything. Every sparrow. Every hair. Every raindrop in last night's downpour. And the Lord doesn't just *know*. He *cares*. He cares deeply. He loves us infinitely and eternally.

Yet if anyone rebels against the Lord's love, He will do everything to change their heart and mind within a yard of hell—except turn them into robots with no heart or mind at all.

---

*Lord, You want courageous men to know
that You know. Yes, You know everything.*

REAL MEN ARE
EMOTIONALLY INTELLIGENT

He [Jesus] looked around at them in anger and,
deeply distressed at their stubborn hearts, said to
the man, "Stretch out your hand." He stretched it
out, and his hand was completely restored.

MARK 3:5

My friend Jonathan is super analytical. Jonathan jokes that until
he and his wife started going to a marriage counselor, he didn't
even know he had emotions. He just thought he was expressing
his thoughts, well, deeply.

Here's some of what I've learned about emotions from Jonathan: *Feeling* emotions is not the same as *having* them. Like
every other human being, you and I have emotions in spades,
but we're not always good at feeling them. You have a couple
of options when it comes to feeling your emotions. You can
choose to feel them now and deal with them in healthy ways
(wise, but not always possible). Or you can choose not to feel
them fully now (wise if you have a realistic and specific future
date for dealing with them in healthy ways).

Thankfully, the Bible shows us plenty of men of faith
expressing emotions. Men like Abraham, Isaac, Jacob, and
Joseph. Men like Moses, Joshua, and Caleb. Men like David
and Asaph. Men like Isaiah, Jeremiah, and Ezekiel. And ultimately, like Jesus, who expressed great joy and righteous anger.
What can you learn from their examples?

---

*Lord, You want courageous men to express
emotions rightly. Please help me, I pray.*

NEVER GIVE UP HOPE

Then the man and his wife heard the sound of the LORD
God as he was walking in the garden in the cool of the day,
and they hid from the LORD God among the trees.

GENESIS 3:8

Imagine standing in the garden of Eden with Adam and Eve.

No, the Lord isn't there for a leisurely walk with the first couple in the cool of the evening. Instead, the three stand by the Tree of Knowledge of Good and Evil.

Adam and Eve had sinned, and they would be ousted from the garden, but the Lord also speaks far into the future about the coming Serpent Crusher (Genesis 3:15). Then He builds an altar, sacrifices a large animal, makes beautiful skins for Adam and Eve, lights a blazing fire, and burns the sacrifice.

Standing not far from the forbidden Tree, the Lord knows He will one day return to make the ultimate sacrifice on another tree. After all, He is the Serpent Crusher.

Sadly, men often tell themselves that the Lord cursed them, but that's not true.

No matter what happens, and no matter how long we must wait, we must remember that Jesus atoned for our sins. God made a way back to paradise.

---

*Lord, You want courageous men to
never give up hope. Thank You for this
vivid reminder of Your love without limits.*

LIVE LIKE AN ELDER

An elder must be blameless, faithful to his wife, a man
whose children believe and are not open to the charge of
being wild and disobedient. Since an overseer manages
God's household, he must be blameless—not overbearing,
not quick-tempered, not given to drunkenness, not
violent, not pursuing dishonest gain.

TITUS 1:6–7

Did you know *every* man of faith is supposed to live like an
elder?

Don't believe me? Read 1 Timothy 3:1–7, Titus 1:5–9, and
1 Peter 5:1–4.

In those key New Testament passages, we're told that
elders care for, shepherd, pastor, lead, and oversee the local
church. While some have official titles, most don't. They live like
an elder regardless of recognition, education, and age.

Living like elders, men of faith learn to teach the Word of
God and its most important truths. They protect the church
from false teachers. They evaluate questions of faith prayer-
fully and carefully.

Just as importantly, they pray for fellow believers, anoint
those who are sick, and visit the imprisoned. They embody the
Good News of Jesus Christ in every sphere of life and maintain
a good reputation in the community.

Again, this isn't for pastors only. This is for *every* man of
faith.

Lord, You want courageous men to live like elders.
When I wrestle with this, help me to say yes.

COURAGE VERSUS RECKLESSNESS, PART 1

The wise are cautious and avoid danger;
fools plunge ahead with reckless confidence.

PROVERBS 14:16 NLT

A mentor once told me that we sense God's presence most when we're most alive. By "alive," he meant when we're out in nature, when we put ourselves at risk, or when we find ourselves in a crisis.

I see myself as a fairly courageous person. The hard part for me is separating courage from recklessness. When I was a teenager, my dad, my brother, and I decided to climb the western slope of Glacier Peak. It was our first climb up this enormous and remote mountain in the North Cascades, but for three of our friends, it was their first time climbing ever.

A couple of days earlier, my dad had dutifully explained all the rules about what to do and—more importantly—what not to do at high altitudes. One of my friends, Jeff, couldn't have acted more bored. In his mind, some of the rules didn't make sense. Like the rule about not resting on large boulders when you're tired. "Don't even go near them," my dad had warned.

To be continued. . .

---

*Lord, You want men to be courageous,
not reckless. Help me know the difference.*

COURAGE VERSUS RECKLESSNESS, PART 2

But they went anyway; recklessly and arrogantly
they climbed to the high hill country.

NUMBERS 14:44 MSG

Two days later, after reaching the top of a particularly large snowfield, Jeff went behind my dad's back over to a car-sized boulder. All he could think of was sitting down.

But Jeff found himself falling headlong beneath eight feet of snow instead. We heard his muffled cries, dug in the soft snow that had caved in above him, and with some difficulty used a rope to pull him back onto hard pack.

My dad was angry. "Jeff, what did I say about going near boulders? They're a magnet for heat from the sun, and they melt the snow around them. Never go near one again. What if we didn't hear you? The snow covered up almost all trace of where you went in. You could have died up here."

The next day when we broke camp, Jeff was still stinging from my dad's words. Carelessly, he didn't tie his sleeping bag securely to the top of his backpack. A couple of hours later, we were walking along the top of a very high ridge, drinking in the spectacular views in all directions, when Jeff's sleeping bag fell off and dropped a hundred feet to our right.

To be continued. . .

Lord, You want courageous men to listen to
wise instruction. Give me ears to hear.

COURAGE VERSUS RECKLESSNESS, PART 3

The words of the reckless pierce like swords.
PROVERBS 12:18

"Go down and get the sleeping bag," I told Jeff. "You have to get it. You'll freeze to death up here tonight without it. Jeff, go down and get it *now*."

He refused, so in my anger I grabbed my ice ax and started making my way down the steep ridge. *That coward*, I thought. *I'm never taking him mountain climbing again.*

As I got close to Jeff's sleeping bag, my heart almost stopped. The sleeping bag had snagged on the smallest of alpine trees on the edge of a sheer cliff that dropped many hundreds of feet in front of me. I was so angry. *That stupid Jeff. Now what am I going to do?*

Get the sleeping bag, of course.

I gripped the snow with my left hand, swung my ice ax for all it was worth, made sure it was secure, reached down, and pulled the sleeping bag from the edge of the cliff.

Now, with no free hand to grip the snow, I had to swing the ice ax above my head—and pray to God that it went in securely.

To be continued. . .

Lord, You want courageous men to think,
then speak, then act. Slow me down, I pray.

COURAGE VERSUS RECKLESSNESS, PART 4

They are surprised that you do not join
them in their reckless, wild living.

1 PETER 4:4

With one hand holding Jeff's sleeping bag, I used the other to swing the ice ax above my head. Then I had to pull myself up as best as I could, create as much friction as possible between my body and the slope, and swing the ice ax again, twelve to eighteen inches at a time, all the way back up to the top.

"There's your stupid sleeping bag, Jeff."

As if it mattered anymore.

My dad just stared at me in anger and disbelief. Earlier, he thought I would come to my senses, stop, and come back. But no, in defiance of every rule in the book, I deliberately risked my life.

For what?

Have you ever put yourself at risk for something trivial and temporal? Maybe something as seemingly important as job security, family harmony, or physical health?

Sometimes it takes the experience of almost destroying our lives to shake up our reckless hearts and minds.

Lord, You want courageous men to abhor
life-and-death risks. Keep me clear minded.

COURAGE VERSUS RECKLESSNESS, PART 5

The younger son gathered all he had and took a journey into a far country, and there he [indulged] in reckless living.

<small>LUKE 15:13 ESV</small>

I loved hiking through the Cascades and Olympic mountains in western Washington state as a young man. I wish I could say I became less reckless over time. Not so.

During our second climb on Glacier Peak, my dad decided to take us up the mountain's largest glacier. It's a 12,500-foot climb, the equivalent of an ant walking up the trunk of a massive western red cedar tree. We had to dig out every handhold and foothold for twelve straight hours until we reached the top of the glacier.

Until that point, we had been staring at hard-packed snow and ice all day without a break to rest, let alone eat. Suddenly, we could look out over the Cascade mountain range. It was breathtaking.

Then came the urgent work of staking our flattened tents as securely as possible before howling winds hit with hurricane force. Anything that wasn't secure blew away. Half the night, I thought that might be our fate as well.

To be continued. . .

Lord, You want courageous men to learn from their mistakes. Keep me from repeating mine.

COURAGE VERSUS RECKLESSNESS, PART 6

They will [remain] reckless, be puffed up
with pride, and love pleasure rather than God.

2 TIMOTHY 3:4 NLT

Morning dawned with a strange quietness. Long before sunrise, a huge cloud cover had swept over the north Cascades. All we could see, besides the top of Glacier Peak above us, were four other mountain peaks in the far distance.

Worse, we quickly realized, the clouds were rising. All plans to reach the summit before lunch were abandoned. Instead, we broke camp and prepared for a rapid descent.

Given the extremely steep slope in front of us, I proposed that our group glissade down the glacier. Picture stepping off a ledge and dropping feetfirst at thirty to forty miles an hour while skiing on your boots.

It would be impossible to fall backward, I argued.

What I should have added: Avoid rolling forward at all costs. Watch out for truck-sized rocks near the bottom of the glacier.

What took twelve hours to ascend took less than five minutes to descend. We dropped 4,650 feet in elevation over 2.35 miles. It was the adrenaline ride of a lifetime.

Afterward, I was told that one false move forward while glissading would have meant almost instant death.

Lord, You want courageous men to shun
reckless adrenaline rushes. Remind me often.

COURAGE VERSUS RECKLESSNESS, PART 7

"The thief comes only to steal and kill and destroy."

JOHN 10:10

Our society seems bent on trying to become more rebellious, more risk-taking, more uninhibited, more outrageous—and less self-controlled. Many blame these trends on the 1960s, but the reality is people have *always* been foolish.

This bent against self-control inevitably hurts our communities, our families, and our friends. Ultimately, it hurts us. Even if it's purely out of self-interest, you and I would do well to decide in our hearts that we want God's help to be self-controlled.

If we lack self-control, then who's in control of our thoughts, speech, and actions? One possibility is we're giving in to the desires of the nature we were born with. That nature's passions and desires are anything but self-controlled.

Another possibility is we are being manipulated or controlled by the devil. If we let Satan control us, he will rob us of everything that's good in our lives. He will tempt us to take risky, dangerous, physically destructive, and even suicidal actions.

---

*Lord, You want courageous men to
abhor recklessness. Please keep me sane.*

GOD WANTS US TO TRULY LIVE

The Lord is not slow in keeping his promise,
as some understand slowness. Instead he
is patient with you, not wanting anyone to
perish, but everyone to come to repentance.

2 PETER 3:9

The last words of the apostle Peter are worth considering. What is utmost on his mind? First, that we keep taking God at His Word, that we cling to it, that we believe what He has said. Second, that we live pure lives, keeping our eyes on eternity—not on what is temporal and soon to fade away. Third, and this is my point here, Peter reminds us that the Lord is patient and doesn't want anyone to perish.

As you've probably already figured out, I did some incredibly stupid things as a young man. None of those actions were motivated by God. It's only by His grace that I lived long enough to do many worthwhile things—like raising a family and serving the Lord.

Even so, someday my body will fail. No amount of vitamins or exercise or medicine or surgery or replacement parts can prevent that from happening. But the Bible says your soul and mine are designed to live forever. And that's a big reason why God doesn't want anyone to perish. He wants us to find true life in Him.

---

*Lord, You want courageous men to
hear Your Word and believe. I believe.*

GOD HONORS COURAGEOUS MEN, PART 1

"Be strong, Take courage. Don't be intimidated.
Don't give them a second thought because GOD,
your God, is striding ahead of you. He's right there
with you. He won't let you down; he won't leave you."

DEUTERONOMY 31:6 MSG

After I gave up mountain climbing, I grew to see myself as a fairly courageous person. Truth is, I still had a long way to go.

While I was studying the life of the prophet Elijah in 1 Kings 17–19, God revolutionized my thinking about courage. The principles I learned then have become second nature to me, lifesavers on many occasions. My prayer is that God will use them to encourage you in a very specific way at this point in your life and for years to come.

In my reading of scripture, I can find no other biblical character (besides Jesus) who shows more courage than Elijah. Elijah was the first man God raised up—a generation after the glory days of King Solomon—to confront the immense wickedness, gross idolatry, and rampant paganism that had consumed Israel.

One lesson we learn from the life of Elijah is that God honors courageous men. . . .

Lord, You want to honor courageous men.
Make me more courageous, I pray.

GOD HONORS COURAGEOUS MEN, PART 2

Now Elijah the Tishbite, from Tishbe in Gilead,
said to Ahab, "As the LORD, the God of Israel,
lives, whom I serve, there will be neither dew nor
rain in the next few years except at my word."

1 KINGS 17:1

When Israel split in two following Solomon's kingship, the northern tribes—which kept the name *Israel*—had a long succession of bad rulers. Ahab, who took the throne as the seventh king of Israel, proved to be viler than any king before him.

Furthermore, his wife was Jezebel, the wicked witch of the north, a Sidonian whose chief ambition in life was to propagate a gross form of paganism in Israel and utterly destroy all worship of the true God. She murdered most of God's prophets, priests, and teachers. If anyone ever was inspired by Satan himself, it was this woman—and her equally wicked husband.

Into this scene stepped Elijah. He pronounced God's judgment on Israel and declared that God was shutting the heavens. Imagine having the audacity to say something like that. It's ludicrous. . .unless God told you to make the announcement.

Still, it required a huge amount of courage to take God at His word, let alone confront King Ahab with such a harsh judgment in the name of the one true God of heaven and earth. But that's exactly what Elijah did.

Lord, You want courageous men to speak
Your words boldly. Increase my faith.

GOD HONORS COURAGEOUS MEN, PART 3

> After a long time, in the third year, the word
> of the LORD came to Elijah: "Go and present
> yourself to Ahab, and I will send rain on the land."
> So Elijah went to present himself to Ahab.

1 KINGS 18:1–2

After pronouncing judgment on the wicked nation of Israel, Elijah headed east across the Jordan River. He did so at the command of God, settling in the wilderness along a brook in the Kerith Ravine, near his hometown of Tishbe.

Later, when the brook dried up, God commanded Elijah to go north to a coastal town in Sidon practically next door to Jezebel's hometown. Again Elijah obeyed God, although this second trip would prove more difficult than the first.

Time passed. God's judgment on Israel had reduced the once prosperous nation to poverty. It hadn't rained in three and a half years. Ahab was absolutely desperate, but he utterly refused to acknowledge the reason for the terrible famine. And he adamantly refused to turn away from his wicked deeds.

Now that Ahab had demonstrated his unrelenting rebellion against God, the Lord told Elijah to go back and confront him once again. Once again, Elijah obeyed.

Lord, You want courageous men to obey
You promptly. Speed up my response times.

GOD HONORS COURAGEOUS MEN, PART 4

The power of the LORD came on Elijah and,
tucking his cloak into his belt, he ran
ahead of Ahab all the way to Jezreel.

1 KINGS 18:46

At God's command, Elijah stepped back into Ahab's life. The king's response when he saw the prophet was to cry out, "Is that you, you troubler of Israel?" (1 Kings 18:17).

Elijah didn't cave under the pressure. He called the people to Mount Carmel for a challenge: the people would set up a sacrifice, and the god who destroyed the sacrifice was truly God. Of course, the false gods of the people did nothing. But the Lord honored Elijah's courage by sending lightning from heaven to devour the sacrifice—altar and all.

Triumphant, Elijah had the prophets of Baal killed, then prayed for and witnessed the end of the drought, before supernaturally beating Ahab's chariot to Jezreel on foot!

Human courage is strongest with the power of God behind it. Biblically, it's difficult to divorce the two. True courage isn't a temperament trait. It's God at work within us, and through us, for His purposes.

But Elijah's courage was about to falter. The queen's schemes had failed, and Jezebel didn't take this lightly. Instead, she vowed to kill the prophet Elijah before another day went by.

Lord, You want courageous men to depend on You for courage and power. I'm depending on You now.

THE OPPOSITE OF COURAGE, PART 1

Elijah was afraid and ran for his life.

1 KINGS 19:3

It's at this point that Elijah proves he's a man just like us.

In a moment of physical weakness (he'd just run a marathon, remember!), Elijah became emotionally distraught over Jezebel's murderous threats. Look at what Elijah did. Instead of crying out to God in prayer and seeking His will, Elijah panicked, went into spiritual neutral, and then hightailed it south into the desert of Beersheba. He even left his servant behind in the rush to save his own skin.

Physically, Elijah became further exhausted. Emotionally, he was completely devastated. Spiritually, he was out of touch with God. Socially, he was utterly isolated.

Vince Lombardi, coach of the Super Bowl–champion Green Bay Packers, once remarked, "Fatigue makes cowards of us all." And it certainly made a coward of Elijah out there in the desert of Beersheba. What's a prophet of God doing in a place like that?

It wasn't until Elijah collapsed under a desert tree in abject despair that he finally remembered to pray. And what a prayer it was! "Lord, I've had enough! Take my life! I feel like dying!" His courage was completely gone—yet his story wasn't over.

Lord, You want courageous men to stay the course.
When I'm tempted to flee, please keep me strong.

THE OPPOSITE OF COURAGE, PART 2

Elijah was as human as we are.

The truth is we're no different than Elijah. We share the same DNA. There are times when even the best of us prove to be cowards. We're vulnerable whenever we're physically exhausted, emotionally upset, spiritually dry, socially isolated.

Think about it. What do you do when the storms of life hit? Immediately pick up the phone and ask someone to pray for you? Open God's Word and ask Him to speak to you? Listen to music to encourage your heart? Get a good night's sleep? Or are you like Elijah? "Woe is me. It doesn't get any worse than this. Just let me die, Lord. I've had enough."

Life is full of circumstances that test our courage. Imminent danger—real or perceived—triggers the strongest of human emotions. Fear is hardwired into our minds. Without thinking, it causes us to shut up, freeze up, even give up. The good news: we can rewire our minds and our responses with a little (or a lot of) help from God.

Lord, You want ordinary men to be made courageous from the inside out. Change how I think so I can act courageously.

THE OPPOSITE OF COURAGE, PART 3

> The angel of the LORD came back a second time and
> touched him [Elijah] and said, "Get up and eat, for the
> journey is too much for you." So he got up and ate and
> drank. Strengthened by that food, he traveled forty days and
> forty nights until he reached Horeb, the mountain of God.
>
> 1 KINGS 19:7–8

Consider how God responded to Elijah at his moment of great-est discouragement and despair. How did God answer his pathetic prayer? Strike him dead? No. Instead, God ministered to Elijah, sending an angel to care for him and put him back on his feet.

Physically, God provided much-needed food and rest. Emotionally, God allowed Elijah to sense His presence. Spiritu-ally, God exhorted Elijah to follow Him again. Socially, God told Elijah that seven thousand other men still followed Him.

Back on his feet, Elijah headed north out of the desert of Beersheba and onto the pages of scripture as one of the great-est heroes of the faith.

Because "Elijah was as human as we are" (James 5:17 NLT), we can learn a great lesson from his response to crisis. Instead of running away, we need to turn to God, trusting that He will respond and meet our needs.

---

*Lord, You never abandon courageous
men of faith. Keep me faithful every day.*

BIBLICAL DEFINITION OF MANHOOD

*"What is mankind that you make so much of them,
that you give them so much attention, that you examine
them every morning and test them every moment?"*

JOB 7:17-18

How does the Bible define manhood? As with many biblical questions, we're often tempted to raise our hands, wave them eagerly, smile big, and answer, "Jesus!"

My good friend Todd Miles, author of *Superheroes Can't Save You*, would be quick to disagree. Jesus wasn't the best of men, or the greatest of men, or the ultimate man. Instead, Jesus was and is fully God and fully man. Imaginary superheroes can't measure up. The greatest biblical heroes can't measure up either.

Then again, I'm so glad many heroes of the faith define manhood with courage and conviction, faith and fortitude, strength and resolve, vibrancy and vitality. They're far from perfect. Together they define the kind of man who follows the Lord wholeheartedly and loves others well, no matter what—until his dying day. That's the kind of man I want to be.

So, how does each biblical hero define manhood? We'll look at twelve examples, starting with Adam and ending with the apostle John.

---

*Lord, You want courageous men to define biblical manhood.
Please give me more backbone and boldness.*

ADAM: WORSHIP YOUR WIFE AND GOD FOR LIFE

> Adam made love to his wife again, and she gave birth to
> a son and named him Seth, saying, "God has granted me
> another child in place of Abel, since Cain killed him."
> Seth also had a son, and he named him Enosh. At that
> time people began to call on the name of the LORD.
>
> GENESIS 4:25–26

In the closing two verses of Adam's life story in the Bible, we see him engaging in two forms of worship: loving his wife and calling on the name of the Lord. Yes, the idea of worshipping your wife may sound strange.

If you're a traditional Anglican, however, you say these words as you place a ring on your bride's finger: "With this ring I thee wed, with my body I thee worship, and with all my worldly goods I thee endow: In the name of the Father, and of the Son, and of the Holy Ghost. Amen."

This idea finds expression in the biblical exhortation, "Rejoice in the wife of your youth. . . . Let her breasts satisfy you always. May you always be captivated by her love" (Proverbs 5:18–19 NLT). It also is celebrated in the Song of Songs.

As Adam illustrates, there's no greater purpose than worshipping your wife and the Lord your God for life.

Lord, You want courageous men to be
faithful for life. I pledge to do just that.

ABRAHAM: BELIEVE WHAT GOD SAYS

> Abram believed the LORD, and he
> credited it to him as righteousness.
>
> GENESIS 15:6

May I offer a different perspective on this verse?

When this famous event took place, what time of day was it? At first, the answer seems obvious. It's the middle of the night, right? Abraham is in his tent praying. The Lord speaks to Abram, as he was called at that point. The two have a little chat. The Lord reinforces His promise and takes Abram outside.

Before the Lord further reinforces His promise, He instructs Abram to do something: "Look up at the sky and count the stars" (Genesis 15:5). Then the Lord adds that pesky phrase, "if indeed you can." As we see in Genesis 18:1—and as we see throughout that region and across southern Europe, southern Asia, and Latin America—many people rest during the hottest part of the day. It turns out that's the best explanation for what time of day it was in verse 5.

In other words, the Lord was saying, in effect: "Abram, I'm asking you to do something that you can't see now. . .but you'll be able to see it tonight, just like almost every other night." Then the Lord adds, "So shall your offspring be."

As Abraham proves, there's no greater faith than believing what God says.

---

*Lord, You want courageous men to believe
what You say. I believe. Help my unbelief.*

JOSEPH: TRUST GOD'S GUIDING HAND

> But Joseph replied, "Don't be afraid of me. Am I God,
> that I can punish you? You intended to harm me, but
> God intended it all for good. He brought me to this
> position so I could save the lives of many people."
>
> GENESIS 50:19–20 NLT

When I decided to become a follower of Jesus Christ, I opened my Bible and began reading. Imagine encountering scripture's most famous stories without any clue what happens next. That was my experience reading God's Word cover to cover for the first time.

By the end of Genesis 44, for instance, I expected Joseph, second only to Pharaoh in Egypt, to tell his armed guards to slaughter his brothers—men who had betrayed their own flesh and blood years earlier. Instead, in the first verses of chapter 45, Joseph barks at his guards, orders them to leave, reveals his true identity to his brothers, and then forgives them. I instantly started weeping. How could I have guessed? I'd never seen that kind of love.

As Joseph's story proves, there's no greater trust than the assurance of God's guiding hand on your life no matter what happens.

---

*Lord, You want courageous men to trust Your
guiding hand. Thanks for Your hand on me.*

MOSES: CELEBRATE THE HOLY SPIRIT IN YOU

But Moses replied, "Are you jealous for my sake?
I wish that all the LORD's people were prophets
and that the LORD would put his Spirit on them!"

NUMBERS 11:29

After Moses complained how hard it was to lead the Israelites, the Lord told him that He would "take some of the power of the Spirit that is on you and put it on them" (Numbers 11:17), referring to seventy elders. At the Lord's instruction, Moses called for the elders. Then God did as He promised.

When Joshua expressed alarm that two of the elders were prophesying among the people, Moses said, in effect, "My wildest dream is that the Lord would put His Spirit on all His people." What a wild dream, indeed!

Of course, that dream came true on the day of Pentecost when every follower of Jesus Christ—both men and women, young and old—received the Holy Spirit's indwelling presence for life (see Acts 2).

What a tremendous gift that every Christian receives from God the Father and His Son, Jesus. Without question, the Holy Spirit resides in every believer.

---

*Lord, You want courageous men to enjoy the
Holy Spirit's presence. What a divine gift!*

SOLOMON: ASK GOD FOR WHOLEHEARTED LOVE

These are the proverbs of Solomon, David's son, king of Israel. . . . Their purpose is to teach people to live disciplined and successful lives, to help them do what is right, just, and fair. These proverbs will give insight to the simple, knowledge and discernment to the young. Let the wise listen to these proverbs and become even wiser. . . . Fear of the LORD is the foundation of true knowledge, but fools despise wisdom and discipline.

PROVERBS 1:1, 3–5, 7 NLT

Near the beginning of his reign, Solomon asked God to give him a discerning heart (1 Kings 3:9). In response, "God gave Solomon wisdom and very great insight, and a breadth of understanding as measureless as the sand on the seashore" (1 Kings 4:29). In time, Solomon was called the wisest man in all the earth (1 Kings 10:23).

If only Solomon had asked for a wholehearted love for the Lord for the rest of his life. As time went on, Solomon compromised and eventually became halfhearted toward the Lord. Being halfhearted isn't sustainable, so eventually Solomon became no-hearted. In that terrible state, Solomon walked away from his devotion to the one true God.

Let's learn from Solomon—and pray to God for a wholehearted love for Him.

---

*Lord, You want courageous men to
wholeheartedly love You. I want to do so too.*

DANIEL: THRIVE IN THE END TIMES

*"Those who are wise will shine like the brightness
of the heavens, and those who lead many to
righteousness, like the stars for ever and ever."*

DANIEL 12:3

Some Bible scholars think we may be living in the end times. If we are, how should we respond? The last chapter in the book of Daniel tells us to be wise and righteous and to lead many others to righteousness. In other words, men of God won't cower in fear. Instead, they will thrive.

You and I should never be surprised by the phenomenal (albeit short-lived) success of evil, Satan-inspired men. Until the climax of history, many evil men will triumph for a time. The twentieth century was no exception. There's no reason to believe the twenty-first century will be an exception either.

But you and I never need to fear that evil men will triumph completely. Why? Because God controls the day they ascend to power and the day of their downfall. This will be true of even the most wicked, Satan-inspired man of all, the Antichrist. God *will* crush His enemies. No matter what happens in years ahead, we need to keep the end of God's story clearly in view—and never lose faith.

---

*Lord, You want courageous men to thrive in the
end times. Keep me from cowering in fear.*

EZRA: TREASURE THE SCRIPTURES

He [Ezra] arrived in Jerusalem on the first day of the fifth month, for the gracious hand of his God was on him. For Ezra had devoted himself to the study and observance of the Law of the LORD, and to teaching its decrees and laws in Israel.

EZRA 7:9–10

Since age thirteen, I have read the Bible cover to cover scores of times, and it never stops enriching me. No wonder I treasure it daily!

I always enjoy reading Ezra 7. That's when Ezra himself steps onto the scene "during the reign of Artaxerxes king of Persia" (verse 1). Ezra's great grandfather, Hilkiah, found the long-lost book of the law written by Moses shortly before the Babylonian captivity. Like Hilkiah, Ezra was both a priest and "a teacher well versed in the Law of Moses, which the LORD, the God of Israel, had given" (verse 6).

Both Jewish and Christian scholars believe Ezra collected, preserved, and curated the Hebrew scriptures during and after the Babylonian captivity. Knowing "the gracious hand of his God was on him" (verse 9), Ezra risked his life to bring the scriptures back to the Promised Land. And Ezra didn't just bring them back; he lived and taught them to the people and led a great revival.

Lord, You want courageous men to treasure the scriptures. May I live in obedience to them today.

NEHEMIAH: DO GREAT WORKS

So on October 2 the wall was finished—just fifty-two
days after we had begun. When our enemies and
the surrounding nations heard about it, they were
frightened and humiliated. They realized this work
had been done with the help of our God.

NEHEMIAH 6:15–16 NLT

When we say, "Solomon built the temple," we don't mean he
did any of the physical work. No, 150,000 other men did that,
though we don't know any of their names.

In contrast, when we say, "Nehemiah rebuilt the walls of
Jerusalem," Nehemiah worked right alongside the laborers
every day—and he even wrote down some of their names.

More importantly, Nehemiah was the answer to his own
fervent, earnest, daily prayers for four straight months. He
knew dreaming great dreams and praying great prayers always
preceded doing great things for God's glory, honor, and praise.
Even Nehemiah's enemies "realized this work had been done
with the help of. . .God" (Nehemiah 6:16 NLT).

Nehemiah's careful, prayerful efforts brought much glory,
honor, and praise to God for many years to come. What an
outstanding legacy in every way.

What great work does God want you to do?

*Lord, You want courageous men to leave a
great legacy. What do You want me to do?*

JOHN THE BAPTIST: FOLLOW THE MESSIAH NO MATTER WHAT

"But for you who fear my name, the Sun of Righteousness will rise with healing in his wings. . . . Look, I am sending you the prophet Elijah before the great and dreadful day of the LORD arrives. His preaching will turn the hearts of fathers to their children, and the hearts of children to their fathers."

MALACHI 4:2, 5–6 NLT

In the final verses of the Old Testament, Malachi quoted the Lord's prophetic words. Those words speak about the coming of (1) the Sun of Righteousness, whom we know as Jesus Christ, and (2) His forerunner, "the prophet Elijah," whom we know as John the Baptist.

Not surprisingly, the angel Gabriel and Jesus Himself compare John the Baptist to the prophet Elijah (Luke 1:17; Matthew 11:13–14; 17:10–13). Unlike Elijah, however, John suffered something unexpected—a cruel death by beheading.

In the middle of Africa I met Tchere, who had survived a gruesome machete attack. When I asked how I could pray for him, Tchere surprised me: "Pray that we might remain firm in our faith in our old age." Then and there I pledged to be that same kind of man.

Lord, You want courageous men to heed the example of John the Baptist. I pledge unfailing allegiance to Jesus Christ.

PETER: READILY CONFESS YOUR SINS

> "But I have prayed for you, Simon,
> that your faith may not fail. And when you
> have turned back, strengthen your brothers."
>
> LUKE 22:32

From the time we were kids, we've been told, "Three strikes and you're out."

In life, we get only so many opportunities to blow it. No wonder our first reaction in many competitive situations is to tense up. Most everyone struggles with the fear of failure, at least occasionally. Every time we hear about another friend or colleague losing his job, we automatically wonder, *Will I be next?*

Thankfully, God's kingdom operates on an entirely different basis. We can never let God down one too many times. If we love Him and own up to our sins, confessing them and asking for His forgiveness, God keeps right on forgiving us and putting us back in the game.

If anyone ever understood the marvel of God's goodness to keep giving second chances, it was Simon Peter. Peter is famous for declaring that he would follow Jesus anywhere—up to the point of death (Luke 22:33)—yet, when put on the spot, he denied even *knowing* Jesus. But as Peter discovered, it's not too late to return to Jesus Christ, confess our sins, ask for His forgiveness, and receive another chance.

Lord, You want courageous men to ask for
forgiveness. I will confess my sins right now.

PAUL: PROTECT THE CHURCH WHEN NEEDED

But even if we or an angel from heaven should preach a gospel other than the one we preached to you, let them be under God's curse!

GALATIANS 1:8

At church today something happened that I'd always heard about but never witnessed before. During a momentary break in the service, a false teacher walked up to the microphone and started speaking. Thankfully, a former lay pastor gently escorted her out of the auditorium, and the service continued.

The apostle Paul easily could have fallen back on his training and rich heritage to embellish the Good News. His whole life before becoming a Christian had been steeped in Jewish learning and tradition, preparing him for the authority and honor of serving as a Pharisee.

But Paul saw clearly the danger of adding anything to the Good News of Jesus Christ. So with the intensity of a jealous husband, Paul took aim at anything that would lead Christians away from their trust in and devotion to the Lord. To protect the purity of the Gospel, Paul argued against false teachers and pleaded with believers.

Like Paul, you and I can preserve the purity of the Gospel through our faith and witness.

Lord, You want courageous men to protect the church from false teachers. When the time comes, may I be ready.

JOHN: LOOK FORWARD
TO ETERNITY WITH JESUS

And I heard a loud voice from the throne saying,
"Behold, the dwelling place of God is with man.
He will dwell with them, and they will be his people,
and God himself will be with them as their God."

REVELATION 21:3 ESV

From the first day the Savior called him to leave his nets, John longed for a deeper friendship with the Lord. To John's delight, Jesus invited him into His closest circle of friends and shared with him moments of brightest glory and deepest grief.

John knew he might die before Jesus returned. But each day of his long life he held on to the *promise* that Jesus would come and the *possibility* that it could be that very day.

Some mornings, John must have scanned the skies, searching for a glimpse of that glorious brightness. One morning he did see the Lord's glory again—transported not by the Lord's return but by the Lord's Spirit as he received the Revelation. What unfolded before John's aged and amazed eyes became his desire and ours as his heart burst out, "Come, Lord Jesus" (Revelation 22:20).

The exclamation point of heaven, after all, isn't the streets of gold. Instead, it's the reality that *God dwells with men*. Like the apostle John, let's look forward to eternity with Jesus!

---

*Lord, You want courageous men to long
to be with You. Yes, come, Lord Jesus!*

EIGHT THINGS TO THINK ABOUT

A person may think their own ways
are right, but the LORD weighs the heart.

PROVERBS 21:2

If you watch futurist movies, you know one of mankind's greatest fears is someone figuring out how to read minds. What we think about defines almost everything else about us. So, what kind of thoughts should fill our minds?

We find the answer in Philippians 4:8: "Finally, brothers and sisters, whatever is true, whatever is noble, whatever is right, whatever is pure, whatever is lovely, whatever is admirable—if anything is excellent or praiseworthy—think about such things."

This verse's eight key words perfectly describe the Lord and His Word and fill the Bible's pages from Genesis 1 to Revelation 22. The eight terms describe a number of biblical heroes as well. Best of all? They can describe you and me.

You might be surprised that many of these biblical heroes are heroines—women both ideal and real. Ideal women like Wisdom and the Virtuous Woman. Real women like Ruth, Rebekah, and Rachel. Yes, it's good to think about them. Notice how frequently their names show up in the days ahead.

---

*Lord, You want courageous men to think carefully
and clearly. Cleanse my thoughts, I pray.*

1. THINK ABOUT WHAT IS TRUE

> When he [Barnabas] arrived and saw what the grace
> of God had done, he was glad and encouraged them
> all to remain true to the Lord with all their hearts.
>
> ACTS 11:23

From the first to the last page of scripture, *true* describes the Lord and everything He says. After all, we're told emphatically that God "does not lie" (Titus 1:2) for "it is impossible for God to lie" (Hebrews 6:18).

But that's not all. The term *true* also describes the thoughts, words, and actions of those who trust God and obey Him. So, *true* can describe you and me and what we aspire to think about, say, and do.

An exceptionally "true" verse: "We know also that the Son of God has come and has given us understanding, so that we may know him who is true. And we are in him who is true by being in his Son Jesus Christ. He is the true God and eternal life" (1 John 5:20). To believe this is to safeguard ourselves from a thousand errors.

My favorite "true" verse: "Jesus answered, 'I am the way and the truth and the life. No one comes to the Father except through me'" (John 14:6).

Lord, You want courageous men to be true in thought, word, and deed. When I veer off course, gently correct me.

2. THINK ABOUT WHAT IS NOBLE

I say of the holy people who are in the land,
"They are the noble ones in whom is all my delight."

PSALM 16:3

The word *noble* describes the Virtuous Woman (Proverbs 12:4; 31:10, 29), Ruth (Ruth 3:11), and Jesus Christ (James 2:7).

The word *noble* also describes the Bereans (Acts 17:11), the work of elders (1 Timothy 3:1), a good-hearted person who receives God's Word and produces a great harvest (Luke 8:15)—and you and me. In everything you and I think, say, and do, we can aspire to be noble.

One of my favorite "noble" verses is Luke 8:15: "But the seed on good soil stands for those with a noble and good heart, who hear the word, retain it, and by persevering produce a crop." May we have noble and good hearts now and always.

My all-time favorite "noble" verse: "But the noble make noble plans, and by noble deeds they stand" (Isaiah 32:8). This is a super easy verse to memorize. Go for it!

---

*Lord, You want courageous men to be noble in
thought, word, and deed. Make me a noble man.*

3. THINK ABOUT WHAT IS RIGHT

> The precepts of the LORD are right, giving joy
> to the heart. The commands of the LORD
> are radiant, giving light to the eyes.
>
> PSALM 19:8

The word *right* and its synonyms appear in almost every book of the Bible, more than 925 times from Genesis 4 to Revelation 22.

Right describes the Lord, His Word, Jesus the "Righteous One," and those who trust God and obey Him, including you and me.

I particularly love these three "right" verses:

"Do what is right and good in the LORD's sight, so that it may go well with you" (Deuteronomy 6:18).

"If you do whatever I command you and walk in obedience to me and do what is right in my eyes by obeying my decrees and commands, as David my servant did, I will be with you" (1 Kings 11:38).

"All the people, even the tax collectors, when they heard Jesus' words, acknowledged that God's way was right" (Luke 7:29).

May you and I do the same!

---

*Lord, You want courageous men to be right
thinkers, teachers, and doers. Lead me in
the ways that are right in Your eyes.*

4. THINK ABOUT WHAT IS PURE

Don't let anyone look down on you because you are
young, but set an example for the believers in speech,
in conduct, in love, in faith and in purity.

1 TIMOTHY 4:12

The word *pure* describes the Lord, the gold in the tabernacle
and temple, and much more (it's especially common in the book
of Job and Psalms). As well, *pure* is one of the first words taught
by Jesus (Matthew 5:8) and is used repeatedly in Paul's writings
to describe devotion to the Lord.

Do you remember the last time you met someone whose
heart clearly was pure? Thanks to our Lord and Savior, Jesus
Christ, we can have the same kind of heart.

That was the apostle Paul's prayer for believers: "And this
is my prayer: that your love may abound more and more in
knowledge and depth of insight, so that you may be able to
discern what is best and may be pure and blameless for the
day of Christ" (Philippians 1:9-10). I encourage you to post that
prayer where you'll see it every day. Pray it from your heart and
you'll be more pure.

---

*Lord, You want courageous men to be pure in thought,
speech, and action. I want that as well.*

5. THINK ABOUT WHAT IS LOVELY

How lovely is your dwelling place, LORD Almighty!

PSALM 84:1

The word *lovely* and its synonyms describe the Lord, the Promised Land, Jerusalem, the tabernacle, the temple, and the New Jerusalem.

Lovely and its synonyms also describe a host of biblical characters: Job's daughters (Job 42:15), Sarah (Genesis 12:11–14), Rebekah (Genesis 24:16; 26:7), Rachel (Genesis 29:17), Moses (Exodus 2:2), David (1 Samuel 16:12), Abigail (1 Samuel 25:3), Bathsheba (2 Samuel 11:2), Tamar and her niece by the same name (2 Samuel 13:1; 14:27), Abishag (1 Kings 1:3–4), Queen Vashti (Esther 1:11), Esther (Esther 2:7), the Two Lovers (Song of Songs 1–7), the herald of Good News (Isaiah 52:7; Romans 10:15), and godly women (1 Peter 3:3–4).

That last entry means I can add my wife, Renée, to the list. Together, we actively worship the Lord for who He is, which is beautiful. What's more, how good that we can thank the Lord daily for His plans, passion, purity, power, providence, and presence in our lives.

---

*Lord, You want courageous men to think
about what is lovely. Today I will think
about the godly people I know.*

6. THINK ABOUT WHAT IS ADMIRABLE

"When she poured this perfume on my body, what she really did was anoint me for burial. You can be sure that wherever in the whole world the Message is preached, what she has just done is going to be remembered and admired."

MATTHEW 26:12–13 MSG

The word *admirable* and its synonyms describe Abel (Hebrews 11:4), Enoch (Hebrews 11:5), Job (Job 29:11), Mary, sister of Martha and Lazarus (Matthew 26:6–13 and John 12:1–8), Paul and Silas (Acts 15:40), Phoebe (Romans 16:1), and elders (Titus 1:7).

Like *true*, *noble*, *right*, *pure*, and *lovely*, *admirable* describes both someone's character and what that person thinks about, says, and does. Each day, may you and I be admirable thinkers. For me, the best way to do that is to start every day with prayer, inspiration, and scripture reading. That's why I enjoy devotional books like this!

The world is awash in fake news, angry tirades, pornographic images, and other warped messages. In all that you and I do, let's stick with what's admirable. "A sensible person wins admiration, but a warped mind is despised" (Proverbs 12:8 NLT).

Lord, You want courageous men to be admirable.
May I be admirable in all I think, say, and do today.

7. THINK ABOUT WHAT IS EXCELLENT

But since you excel in everything—in faith, in speech, in knowledge, in complete earnestness and in the love we have kindled in you—see that you also excel in this grace of giving.

2 CORINTHIANS 8:7

The word *excellent* and its synonyms describe Wisdom (Proverbs 3:13–20; 8:1–35), the Virtuous Woman (Proverbs 31:10), and Ruth (Ruth 3:11). It can also describe you and me, especially if God's life and love flow in and through us.

An "excellent" verse appears right before the Bible's Love Chapter, 1 Corinthians 13: "And yet I will show you the most excellent way" (1 Corinthians 12:31).

And here are two more "excellent" verses for every man:

"A deacon must be faithful to his wife and must manage his children and his household well. Those who have served well gain an excellent standing and great assurance in their faith in Christ Jesus" (1 Timothy 3:12-13).

"I want you to stress these things, so that those who have trusted in God may be careful to devote themselves to doing what is good. These things are excellent and profitable for everyone" (Titus 3:8).

Lord, You want courageous men to be excellent in thought, word, and action. May I excel more and more.

8. THINK ABOUT WHAT IS PRAISEWORTHY

We will tell the next generation the praiseworthy deeds of
the LORD, his power, and the wonders he has done.

PSALM 78:4

The word *praiseworthy* and its synonyms describe the Virtuous
Woman (Proverbs 31:30), Ruth (Ruth 2:11-12), and you and me—
especially if we develop praiseworthy character, genuineness,
and integrity.

We may find it difficult, but God wants us to be immune
to the world's applause and to live every moment filled with
the Holy Spirit, just like Jesus. Thankfully, His Spirit continually
resides within us (Romans 8:9). It's not a matter of getting more
of the Holy Spirit. Instead, it's a matter of surrendering more
and more pieces of our heart and life to Him. When I'm most
courageous, I ask God to gently and clearly reveal which pieces
I'm holding back.

As Philippians 4:8 says, let's actively and wholeheartedly
choose to think about what is true, noble, right, pure, lovely,
admirable, excellent, and praiseworthy. If we do, our thoughts
and actions will eventually reveal our Christlike character to a
watching world.

---

*Lord, You want courageous men to be praiseworthy
in Your eyes. That's my goal every day.*

LOVE WIDOWS

A father to the fatherless, a defender
of widows, is God in his holy dwelling.

PSALM 68:5

How often does the topic of widows come up in the Bible? Surprisingly, a lot! The most famous widow's story is found at the end of Mark 12. On first reading, we might wonder why Jesus approved of a poor woman giving "all she had to live on" (verse 44). Of course, He knew that God would provide for her needs. But God often provides through the giving of His other children—like you and me.

Early in our marriage, Renée and I were asked to lead our first home Bible study. When we said yes, we were asked who we wanted in our group. We looked at each other and said, "That's easy. We want a living room full of widows." That was an amazing, wonderful year full of wisdom as we learned from nearly a dozen godly, lovely, and loving widows.

Sadly, not everyone loves widows. The Sadducees and other religious leaders controlled the judicial system, which barred women. When a woman's husband died, therefore, she couldn't do anything to protect her family's property from being seized. How wicked. Jesus condemned these religious scam artists in no uncertain terms (Mark 12:38–40).

Lord, You want courageous men to love widows.
Which widow do You want me to love today?

HELP POOR WIDOWS

> Be joyful at your festival—you, your sons and
> daughters. . .and the Levites, the foreigners, the
> fatherless and the widows who live in your towns.
>
> DEUTERONOMY 16:14

In biblical times, loving your neighbor meant giving to the poor on a regular basis, especially widows. How?

First, by providing food and clothing (Deuteronomy 10:18) and inviting them to join your family for every holiday feast (Deuteronomy 16:10–14).

Second, by sharing part of your wealth with them every third year (Deuteronomy 14:28–29; 26:12–13).

Third, by leaving part of your crops for them to glean during each harvest (Deuteronomy 24:19–21). We see this intricately woven into the story of Ruth, who, after her husband's death, temporarily experienced homelessness and poverty and went to glean in Boaz's fields.

Jesus and His disciples gave alms to the poor regularly. It's what all godly, good-hearted Jewish people did. Sadly, however, the poor widow of Mark 12 had been neglected by relatives and overlooked by neighbors. All she had left were two small coins.

---

*Lord, You want courageous men to help poor widows.
Which widow do You want me to help today?*

NEVER OVERLOOK POOR WIDOWS

Jesus sat down opposite the place where the offerings
were put and watched the crowd putting their money
into the temple treasury. Many rich people threw in
large amounts. But a poor widow came and put in two
very small copper coins, worth only a few cents.

MARK 12:41–42

I can imagine the poor widow of Mark 12 contemplating the
promises of God as she walks toward the temple that Tuesday,
just three days before our Lord Jesus gave His all for us on the
cross.

As she walks into the court in front of the temple, I can
imagine the widow carefully carrying her small purse, contemplating what she is about to do. As Jesus watches, she stops in
front of a funnel-shaped offering receptacle. She reaches out
her hand and drops in her last two small bronze coins.

Jesus knew this widow well—He knows all widows. And He
knew this poor widow had no property and no close family to
take care of her. Therefore, since it was something He did often,
I also imagine that Jesus motioned for one of His disciples to
follow after her and quietly give her a handful of silver coins.

*Lord, You want courageous men to give generously
to poor widows. Which widow needs help today?*

LEARN FROM THE POOR WIDOW

Calling his disciples to him, Jesus said, "Truly I tell you, this poor widow has put more into the treasury than all the others. They all gave out of their wealth; but she, out of her poverty, put in everything—all she had to live on."

MARK 12:43–44

Consider what this poor widow shows us.

First, she shows us that *no gift is too large*.

Jesus tells us that she put in more than all the other contributors. She put in all she had to live on. Of course, she could do this because she wasn't obligated to care for anyone else. Scripture teaches that our obligation to care for our family's real needs supersedes any gift we desire to give. Giving isn't a way to shirk our God-given responsibilities at home.

Second, she shows us that *no gift is too small*.

Her two coins couldn't even buy the smallest bird to eat or sacrifice. How in the world could her miniscule donation make any difference? To Jesus, it made all the difference in the world. That small donation proved that this poor widow was fully and wholly dedicated to the Lord her God. I'm moved by her love, trust, and sheer bravery. And she clearly moved Jesus, whose words in Mark 12 honor her.

Lord, You want men to be courageous in their giving.
How much do You want me to give this week?

HEED THE POOR WIDOW'S EXAMPLE

"Where your treasure is, there your heart will be also."
MATTHEW 6:21

How easily we ignore this marvelous truth: everything—
everything—we desire, want, and need is found in the Lord and
through the Lord alone. You can be sure this marvelous truth
had grabbed hold of the heart of the poor widow in Mark 12. As
a result, she gave all she had. In times of need, are we willing
to do the same?

Imagine you have only eighty dollars left to pay eight hundred dollars of bills. Or imagine getting so low you have only
two pennies to your name. What's the only thing a wholehearted lover of God can do? Yes, put it in the offering. Give
it all. Don't hold anything back. And then don't be surprised
when God blesses you with a handful of silver coins. Don't be
surprised when God blesses you with an anonymous gift of
810 dollars. Not 800, but 810, because God remembered that
you also needed some gas money.

Yes, the Lord's providential work and His answers to our
specific prayers do something wonderful. They increase our
love, faith, and trust in Him.

How sad when personal interests, wants, and desires end
up squeezing someone's offerings to a trickle.

---

*Lord, You want men to be courageous givers in
their times of financial need. You know my finances.
Help me know how much to give You this week.*

GIVE YOURSELF
WHOLEHEARTEDLY TO GOD

And they exceeded our expectations:
They gave themselves first of all to the Lord,
and then by the will of God also to us.

2 CORINTHIANS 8:5

I recently met a couple who have increased their monthly giving by 20 percent. I was introduced to another couple who have doubled their church giving. Yet another couple, when doing their taxes, realized they had given away the equivalent of the wife's entire annual salary to their church and missionaries. She quipped, "Why in the world did I land such a demanding job?" Yet God has richly blessed them!

The apostle Paul unpacks a life-changing truth in 2 Corinthians 8, especially verse 5: generous giving is the outflow of all who give themselves "first of all to the Lord."

Every morning I tell God, *Today I want to love You wholeheartedly! And today I want to love others well. May I experience, and overflow with, Your love.*

How is your heart? Filled with love for God and others? Overflowing in giving? I hope so!

---

*Lord, You want courageous men to give You
their all. I give myself fully to You again today.*

JESUS HEADS NORTH

Jesus left that place and went to the vicinity of Tyre. He entered a house and did not want anyone to know it; yet he could not keep his presence secret. In fact, as soon as she heard about him, a woman whose little daughter was possessed by an impure spirit came and fell at his feet. The woman was a Greek, born in Syrian Phoenicia.

MARK 7:24–26

Jesus did a lot of talking during His earthly ministry. At certain times, however, Jesus was best known for His silence.

One day Jesus told His disciples that they were going to head north out of the Promised Land and into the region of Tyre and Sidon. He specifically said He wanted His presence kept secret, but the word got out. It always gets out. Soon the house where they were staying no longer was a quiet oasis. So, Jesus went for a walk around town.

I can imagine that, to the disciples, the walk felt aimless. Jesus wasn't talking. He just kept walking, going this way and then that. Around one corner, Jesus stopped. Down the street a woman waved her hands in the air, shouted praises, hurriedly came up to them, and fell at Jesus' feet: "Lord, Son of David, have mercy on me!" she said (Matthew 15:22).

To be continued. . .

Lord, You want courageous men to follow
You anywhere. Today, I trust Your leading.

JESUS DOESN'T SAY A WORD

Jesus did not answer a word. So his disciples
came to him and urged him, "Send her away,
for she keeps crying out after us."

MATTHEW 15:23

The woman cried out, and Jesus stunned everyone by not saying anything.

The disciples, much like many people today, couldn't stand quiet, so after the initial awkward silence of Jesus, they started talking. Of course, they had no idea what to say, so they started berating the Syrian woman. By the end, they were telling Jesus to send her away. *If You can't help her, at least get her out of here. A crowd is forming. This looks bad.*

The woman kept repeating her affirmation of faith and desperate plea for the healing of her demon-possessed daughter.

Still, Jesus said nothing. A minute passed. Maybe two.

I can imagine the disciples continuing to fill the air with their words, or perhaps standing uncomfortably silent beside Jesus.

So, what was Jesus doing? Was He punishing the woman? To be continued. . .

---

*Lord, You want courageous men to pay
attention to what You don't say. I'm listening.*

JESUS SPEAKS TO THE HEART

The woman came and knelt before him.
"Lord, help me!" she said.

MATTHEW 15:25

Sometimes what Jesus says or does makes us cringe. But we can trust that He is never a hypocrite and that He is always loving.

In Jewish culture during Jesus' day, religious men in public places typically didn't give women more than a fleeting glance. To do anything else was shameful, even scandalous. Yet I can imagine Jesus looking into the woman's eyes, eyes which see something in His gaze that she had never seen before. No one had ever looked at her with such love, respect, compassion, and confidence.

Before Jesus breaks His silence, let us note that it appears the Syrian woman loves Him. For the first time—in her heart and evidenced in her countenance—she is worshipping the One she has always longed for.

So, when Jesus finally did break His silence, the woman had faith in what Jesus was going to do next.

To be continued. . .

Lord, You want courageous men to look
with empathy. I want to see others that way.

JESUS REBUKES HIS DISCIPLES

He answered, "I was sent only
to the lost sheep of Israel."

MATTHEW 15:24

"Don't you know?" Jesus said—not to the woman, but to the disciples. "Don't you know that I was sent only to the *lost* sheep of the house of Israel?" Twelve of the lost Jewish sheep standing there probably gulped hard. Jesus was rebuking the disciples in no uncertain terms.

Then Jesus turned back to the woman and said, "Woman, don't you know it isn't right to take the children's bread and throw it to the dogs?" I can imagine Him smiling ever more exuberantly and the woman laughing. Far from offended, she plays along.

"Yes, Lord," she said for all to hear, "but the children themselves drop scraps and crumbs to their pet dogs under the table."

Then, so there was no mistake, Jesus said, "For such a reply, you may go; the demon has left your daughter" (Mark 7:29). Jesus adds: "Woman, you have great faith! Your request is granted" (Matthew 15:28).

I can see the crowd cheering with gusto. *We thought Jesus couldn't help her, but He did.*

To be continued. . .

---

*Lord, You want courageous men to recognize
the errors of their way. I'm not always right.*

WHAT WAS JESUS DOING?

She went home and found her child
lying on the bed, and the demon gone.

MARK 7:30

The only ones not cheering at Jesus' pronouncement were the chagrined and disgraced disciples, but they would never treat a woman or Gentile like that again.

Imagine if Jesus had started talking the moment the Syrian woman begged for His help. Yes, that would have been the polite thing to do. Or He could have walked away. Yet Jesus did neither.

True, Jesus still could have healed her daughter. . .but everything else would have been lost. In Jesus' eyes, it was more important to win and heal and bless the woman. It was more important to grant her heart's true desire. It was more important to honor and respect her for all to see.

In reality, every person in that crowd had a choice to make after witnessing the scene. *Am I for Jesus—or against Him? Do I trust His heart—or hate Him?*

We face the same questions. And the choice is clear.

Lord, You want courageous men to trust Your heart at all times. I promise to trust You today.

DON'T FREEZE UP, PART 1

"He asked them, 'Why have you been
standing here all day long doing nothing?'"
MATTHEW 20:6

We all know what fear feels like. It feels terrible. It's the knot in our stomach. It's the squeeze of our throat. It's the sweat beading on us. It's the sudden pounding headache. It's the feeling we're about to throw up.

When fear grips us, we're hardwired for fight, flight, or freeze.

My good friend Mike knows all about the latter. At one point after he made a career change, I served as one of Mike's mentors. An unexpected disappointment hit Mike and he froze up. Mike couldn't take the next necessary step to move his big project forward. That's often what happens when our hearts are gripped by one of the five professional fears (fear of silence, fear of sharing, fear of selling, fear of rejection and failure, and fear of success).

I knew exactly what Mike needed to do next. Thanks to my mentoring, he knew it too. Still, I made the mistake of thinking Mike could unfreeze on his own, but that didn't happen the first week. Or the second. Or the third. . .

Lord, You don't want courageous men
to freeze up. Please help me get unstuck.

DON'T FREEZE UP, PART 2

They said nothing to anyone,
because they were afraid.

MARK 16:8

Finally, I picked up the phone and called my friend's bluff.

"Mike?"

"Hey, David. What's up?"

"What's up?" I asked sarcastically. "What's up?" I asked again even more sarcastically. "You're a filthy dog. [Long pause.] Your wife is ugly. [Even longer pause.] Your kids are pathetic—"

I was just warming up when Mike cut me off.

"Okay, okay," he yelled, half in shock and half laughing. "You can lay off. I promise: I'm unfrozen. I'll get back in action first thing tomorrow."

Did you catch how time efficient this approach is? And contrary to what you might think, this approach also expresses the deepest degree of friendship, trust, and love. Otherwise, I could *never* say such things to Mike.

When fear grips us, we're hardwired for fight, flight, or freeze. We're also hardwired for one more response: focus.

---

*Lord, You want courageous men to learn
to focus on foundational biblical truths.
Teach me to do just that in the days ahead.*

FOCUS ON FOUNDATIONAL
BIBLICAL TRUTHS, PART 1

Guide me in your truth and teach me, for you are God
my Savior, and my hope is in you all day long.

Psalm 25:5

True courage focuses on the foundational truths found in God's
Word. These foundational truths deal with who God really is,
then who you are as a follower of Jesus Christ, and finally how
life works.

Believe me, I clearly remember when God destroyed my
previous theology of how life works—and then replaced it with
a new, much more robust theology that squares with the Bible's
teachings.

Not every Christian is innately brave and courageous. I discovered that to my shock at age twenty-four. My new bride,
Renée, and I had known each other for a full decade before we
married. We knew *everything* about each other. That certainly
seemed to be the case at every turn during our honeymoon. It
wasn't until the two of us settled into everyday life that I learned
something unexpected: my wife struggled with courage. Within
months, however, that changed completely, and she's out-
couraged me ever since.

To this day, Renée and I keep experiencing courage. More
importantly, we show others the steps to true courage. That's a
key reason why I'm writing this devotional book!

---

*Lord, You want courageous men to focus
on Your truth. That's my desire as well.*

FOCUS ON FOUNDATIONAL BIBLICAL TRUTHS, PART 2

The LORD is near to all who call on him,
to all who call on him in truth.

PSALM 145:18

I've learned not to make the mistake of trying to jump from fear straight to true courage. Instead, I work on my focus. You can too. It won't eliminate fear, but it will give you the courage you need for today.

Toward that end, I repeat these foundational biblical truths every day, and I invite you to do the same.

1. I pray the Lord's Prayer found in Matthew 6:9–13. From time to time I change the Bible translation to keep it fresh.

2. I thank the Lord for the apostle Paul's words in 1 Corinthians 15:58 (NLT): "Be strong and immovable. Always work enthusiastically for the Lord, for you know that nothing you do for the Lord is ever useless."

3. I pray, "Lord, when it comes to knowing, loving, trusting, following, and obeying You, I want to be nothing less than wholehearted!"

4. I pray, "Lord, I want to experience and overflow with a renewal of Your love."

5. I thank the Lord for Paul's words in Galatians 5:6 (NLT): "What is important is faith expressing itself in love."

---

*Lord, You want courageous men to focus on
Your truth daily. Today I'm going to do just that.*

FOCUS ON FOUNDATIONAL BIBLICAL TRUTHS, PART 3

Love does not delight in evil
but rejoices with the truth.

1 CORINTHIANS 13:6

Every day, I repeat five more foundational biblical truths. Again, I think of them as the way I focus at the start of each day. I invite you to do the same.

6. I thank the Lord for Luke 2:52, which says that God's Son, Jesus, is loved by God the Father and by all who know Him. I then affirm: If I know and love Jesus as He really is, I am a blessed man, indeed!

7. I pray, "Lord, Your providential work and Your answers to my specific prayers increase my faith and trust in You!"

8. I thank the Lord for John 17:23, which says that God the Father loved the disciples as much as He loved Jesus. How incredibly blessed they were!

9. I pray, "How very good that I can thank You daily, Lord, for Your sovereignty (greatness), providence (guidance and goodness), holiness (glory), love (graciousness), and mystery ("God alone knows").

10. I thank the Lord for Lamentations 3:24, which says my most prized possession is the Lord in my life.

---

*Lord, You want courageous men to focus
on key biblical truths daily. May I always
affirm the truths You provide in Your Word.*

FOCUS ON FOUNDATIONAL BIBLICAL TRUTHS, PART 4

Instead, speaking the truth in love, we will grow
to become in every respect the mature body
of him who is the head, that is, Christ.

EPHESIANS 4:15

Every day, I repeat still more foundational biblical truths, and I invite you to do the same.

11. I pray, "Everything I desire, want, and need is found in You, Lord, and through You alone. Why should I look anywhere else?"

12. I thank the Lord for 2 Corinthians 12:9, which says that God's gracious favor is all I need and that His power works best in my frailty and weaknesses.

13. I thank the Lord for Psalm 73:25–26 (NLT): "Whom have I in heaven but you? I desire you more than anything on earth. My health may fail, and my spirit may grow weak, but God remains the strength of my heart; he is mine forever."

14. I pray, "Lord, I thank You for Your providence and pray for Your good provision so I love You wholeheartedly and love others well."

15. I pray, "Lord, You know the number of my days. May I bring You glory, honor, and praise."

---

*Lord, You want courageous men to focus on
foundational biblical truths daily. Help me to
know them by heart, and pray them in my spirit.*

OVERCOME THE TOP PROFESSIONAL FEARS, PART 1

The LORD is my light and my salvation—
whom shall I fear? The LORD is the stronghold
of my life—of whom shall I be afraid?

PSALM 27:1

You may be an entertainer taking home thirty-five thousand dollars per hour. You may be a pitcher for the Boston Red Sox. You may be a Wall Street corporate merger guru. Still. . .

You and I have to understand, quickly recognize, and know how to defeat the top professional fears.

Not surprisingly, most (not all) successful individuals initially assume they are the exception to the rule. "Fear? Who me? No way."

"No fear" isn't just a motto for the adventurous. It's a way of life. I know all this, yet the other day I got hit with one of the five professional fears and responded 180 degrees opposite of what I know to do in such situations.

I still believe "No fear" is a way of life, but it's an imperfect way. Every time we give in to fear, we need to humbly acknowledge it and remind ourselves what to do next time.

---

*Lord, You want courageous men to defeat
temporal fears. Teach me how to overcome fear.*

OVERCOME THE TOP PROFESSIONAL FEARS, PART 2

The fear of the LORD is the beginning of wisdom,
and knowledge of the Holy One is understanding.

PROVERBS 9:10

Over the years I've identified five top professional fears. Today, let's look at the first.

Number one: *The fear of silence* is seen in our obsession with all things digital. We always seem to be scrolling, posting, texting, talking. . . . Ironically, without silence, we can't truly know ourselves, let alone tap into our amazing gifts of intuition, deduction, creativity, and more.

Want to test yourself? Ask a room full of people to put away all things electronic and all reading materials, to stop all conversations and looking around, and to simply remain silent for five minutes. Often, you will discover that you can't wait out those five minutes. Test yourself over and over until you can do it. Then move to ten minutes. Then to fifteen minutes.

If you master this in front of a room full of people, you'll be well on your way to mastering it when you're alone. In time, your natural gifts of intuition, deduction, and creativity will begin to take flight.

---

*Lord, You want courageous men to defeat
the fear of silence. Help me to rest in You.*

OVERCOME THE TOP PROFESSIONAL FEARS, PART 3

The wise fear the LORD and shun evil,
but a fool is hotheaded and yet feels secure.

PROVERBS 14:16

Let's look at the next two professional fears.

Number two: *The fear of sharing* takes us all the way back to grade school.

In kindergarten, we freely and sometimes enthusiastically share our artwork with the teacher, our classmates, and our family. By third or fourth grade, however, we lock in on the fact that our sharing isn't always received the way we expected.

And we take that fear with us into adulthood. Don't give in to those irrational fears—thoughts like "a friend may steal my idea if I tell her" or "a colleague might think my idea is stupid." The biggest and best ideas thrive in an atmosphere of camaraderie.

Number three: *The fear of selling.* And not just in a professional sales sense. It is seen in our reluctance to invite others to teach us, mentor us, assist us, encourage us, strengthen us, and open doors for us.

These fears are common, but they stifle what God wants to do in our lives. He will help us to overcome them.

---

*Lord, You want courageous men to reach out to others.
Help me today to both give and receive.*

OVERCOME THE TOP PROFESSIONAL FEARS, PART 4

Wisdom's instruction is to fear the LORD,
and humility comes before honor.

PROVERBS 15:33

Let's look at the last two professional fears.

Number four: *The twin fears of rejection and failure* are well-known and covered extensively in other books, so I'll keep moving. . . .

Number five: When I bring up *the fear of success*, people laugh almost every time. Yes, it sounds completely backward. Why would anyone fear something positive? But fear doesn't always make sense—it's not always rational. So, tell the truth: Do you want to be successful? If so, great! If not, what are your other options? I'll take success any day. I hope you will too!

Make a list of these five professional fears. Remember, you'll give in to them from time to time. That's okay. Just promise yourself that you'll always get right back to doing what the Lord has called you to do in the world of work.

Lord, You want courageous men to succeed.
Empower me to walk in Your ways.

WHAT GOD SAYS ABOUT FEAR, PART 1

The people feared the LORD
and put their trust in him.

EXODUS 14:31

Every time we give in to fear, we need to humbly acknowledge it and remind ourselves what to do next time. This is true in every sphere of life, not just work, and it all begins with a biblical understanding of who the Lord our God is and what He has to say about fear. God hates cowardice, but He also despises bravado. So. . .

How does the Lord want us to live?

1. Fear the Lord, which is the beginning of true wisdom (Job 28:28, Psalm 111:10, Proverbs 1:7; 9:10; 15:33).

2. Fear the Lord and do what He says (Deuteronomy 10:12, Ecclesiastes 12:13, Philippians 2:12).

3. Take courage in the Lord again today (Joshua 1:9, 1 Chronicles 28:20, Haggai 2:4, John 16:33, 1 John 5:4–5).

4. Encourage others to continue trusting the Lord (Numbers 14:6–9, Deuteronomy 31:6, 1 Corinthians 16:13, 1 Timothy 6:11–12).

Lord, You want courageous men to fear You and encourage others. Use me to encourage someone else today.

WHAT GOD SAYS ABOUT FEAR, PART 2

"Oh, that their hearts would be inclined to fear
me and keep all my commands always, so that it
might go well with them and their children forever!"

DEUTERONOMY 5:29

How else does the Lord want us to live?

5. Trust the Lord continually without wavering or doubting (1 Kings 18:21, Psalm 26:1, Matthew 21:21, Mark 9:24, Romans 4:20–22, Hebrews 10:23, Jude 21).

6. Trust the Lord by continually doing what is good and right (2 Corinthians 1:24, Galatians 5:6, Philippians 1:25, Colossians 2:7, 2 Thessalonians 1:3, James 2:14).

7. Trust the Lord and do not fear what others might do (2 Chronicles 20:15, Nehemiah 4:14, Psalm 118:6, Isaiah 41:10, Matthew 10:28).

8. Trust the Lord no matter what is happening (Romans 5:3, 2 Corinthians 6:4, 2 Thessalonians 1:4–5, 2 Timothy 2:3, Hebrews 10:35–36, James 1:3; 5:11, 1 Peter 1:6–7; 5:8–11, Revelation 2:10).

Make a list of these eight ways the Lord wants us to live, and carry it with you. Remember, you'll fail from time to time. That's okay. Just promise yourself that you'll always get right back to living the way the Lord has called you to live.

---

*Lord, You want courageous men to
keep trusting You. Help me fear only You.*

BLESSED BY GOD'S PRESENCE, PART 1

You make known to me the path of life;
you will fill me with joy in your presence.

PSALM 16:11

Have you ever seen a large room light up the moment a famous person enters? You can feel the electricity racing to every corner of the room. There is something intangible yet very real about their magnetism. Their larger-than-life persona mysteriously charges you and changes you; it makes you want to capture even a momentary smile from them. In a word, you feel *blessed*.

That's an inadequate picture of what it can be like to be in the presence of God. Here is the first of six truths about God's presence that are taught in scripture.

1. God's presence is everywhere. This is sometimes called God's omnipresence. In Psalm 139:7–12, David said God already is everywhere we might go in this life and the next. The prophet Jeremiah said God fills the heavens and earth (Jeremiah 23:23–24). This amazing truth is based on the fact that the Lord God created the entire universe and is so much, much greater than the heavens and earth. The universe is but a small drop of dew or a tiny white wildflower. Of course, size doesn't matter. God is both outside and inside His marvelous creation.

Lord, You want courageous men to enjoy Your presence. Help me learn to enjoy it here and now.

BLESSED BY GOD'S PRESENCE, PART 2

Blessed are those who have learned to acclaim you,
who walk in the light of your presence, LORD.

PSALM 89:15

Here are three more biblical truths about God's presence.

2. *God's presence fills heaven* with His infinite and eternal glory, majesty, power, dominion, holiness, and love. The angels of heaven stand in His presence with awe and worship and rejoicing. So do believers from Adam and Eve to our loved ones who have gone to be with the Lord. We never pray to them, but they continue to pray to the Lord God (Revelation 5:8; 8:3–4).

3. *God's presence fills the earth.* We learn this from the Lord Himself in Numbers 14:21, from David in Psalm 8:1, from the seraphim in Isaiah 6:3, and from the Lord again in both Isaiah 11:9 and Habakkuk 2:14.

4. *God's presence takes up residence in every Christian.* In fact, Romans 8:9 and other scriptures teach that if the Spirit of God isn't in someone, that person isn't a Christian yet.

Thankfully, you can experience God's presence throughout your life. It's not one-and-done. Heaven alone is proof of that!

---

*Lord, You want courageous men to rejoice
in Your presence within them. Thank You!*

BLESSED BY GOD'S PRESENCE, PART 3

"Now we are all here in the presence of God to listen to everything the Lord has commanded you to tell us."

ACTS 10:33

Here is another important biblical truth about God's presence.

5. *God can reveal His presence to anyone in any manner He chooses.* We see this with Moses (burning bush) and Aaron (budding staff). We see this with Elijah (gentle whisper). We also see this when God sent an angel to the Roman centurion Cornelius (Acts 10–11). Ultimately, we see this when God sent His own Son, Jesus Christ.

This truth is why there are innumerable reports of God appearing to people all over the world today, typically in their dreams. While God commands us to proclaim the Gospel of Jesus Christ to everyone in every nation, God hasn't tied His own hands. Instead, He's winning people to Jesus Christ every day in every country on this planet. He's making sure the wedding feast of the Lamb will be joyous beyond measure.

Are there people you know who need God to reveal His presence to them? Why not pray for them today?

_____

*Lord, You want courageous men to pray
for others who need Your presence in their
lives. Today I want to pray for _____.*

BLESSED BY GOD'S PRESENCE, PART 4

How can we thank God enough for you in return for all the
joy we have in the presence of our God because of you?

1 THESSALONIANS 3:9

We can't finish talking about God's presence without considering one more important biblical truth.

6. *When God reveals His presence to you, you'll know it.*
Remember the electricity that races through us when someone famous walks by? Ditto when God draws near. When God
draws near to you, imagine Him looking right at you—smiling.
That's one of the best ways to feel blessed, isn't it? These experiences are sometimes called moments of *transcendence*.

You can't predict when God will make His presence known.
It could be at a church service, citywide prayer gathering, or
Christian concert. It could be while you're walking outside,
looking up at the night sky, or watching a magnificent sunrise
or sunset. Then again, it could be when you're working, doing
God's will, or spending time with dear Christian friends.

Not knowing when you'll feel God's presence should *encourage* you. It should encourage you to think about God, meditate on these truths, and pay attention to what you're feeling.
Then in moments of transcendence, praise Him!

---

*Lord, You want courageous men to experience
Your presence. When I do, I will praise You!*

QUICK FACTS ABOUT GOD'S PRESENCE, PART 1

> The LORD replied, "My Presence will
> go with you, and I will give you rest."
>
> EXODUS 33:14

Here are four fast but important facts about God's presence.

1. Adam and Eve's son Cain was the first man to walk out from the Lord's presence (Genesis 4:16).
2. Isaac was the first patriarch to link the Lord's presence and blessings (Genesis 27:7). This theme runs throughout the Law (Exodus 33:14, 19; Deuteronomy 12:7, 18; 14:23, 26; 27:7) and throughout the New Testament (Acts 2:28, 1 Thessalonians 3:9).
3. Moses was the first prophet to enter the Lord's presence to speak with Him (Exodus 34:34). This was a picture of divine mission, strength, and courage.
4. Aaron was the first high priest to enter the Lord's presence in the tabernacle (Exodus 28:30). This was a picture of service and of entering God's presence in heaven.

Lord, You want courageous men to live conscious of Your presence. Thank You so much for being in my life.

QUICK FACTS ABOUT GOD'S PRESENCE, PART 2

How precious to me are your thoughts, God! How vast is the sum of them! Were I to count them, they would outnumber the grains of sand—when I awake, I am still with you.

Here are three more fast but important facts about God's presence.

1. As kings, both David and Solomon linked the Lord's presence and prayer (1 Kings 8:28, 2 Chronicles 6:19, Psalm 139). We see this reiterated in Ephesians 3:12 and Hebrews 10:22.
2. In scripture, the Lord repeatedly equates His judgment with removal from His presence and blessing. We see this in many Old Testament passages, such as 2 Kings 17:18–23, Isaiah 2:19–21 and 3:8, and Jeremiah 52:3. Jumping to the New Testament, we see this again in Matthew 25:41–46 and 2 Thessalonians 1:9.
3. The apostle Paul linked the Lord's presence and His second coming in 1 Thessalonians 2:19 and 3:13 and 2 Timothy 4:1.

Lord, You want courageous men to enjoy Your presence. I rejoice that Your home is within me.

REASONS AND WAYS TO SEEK GOD, PART 1

Seek the LORD while he may be found;
call on him while he is near.

ISAIAH 55:6

History, literature, and science tell many stories of heroic yet not always successful quests, journeys, struggles, and searches.

In the past three generations, the whole world has been galvanized by particular races. One was the race to space—to the moon, to Mars, and beyond. Another was the race to cyberspace—to the internet, to the World Wide Web, and beyond. The first allowed humans to leave earth. The second allowed humans around the planet to communicate with each other instantly and to access knowledge freely.

Like history, literature, and science, the Bible tells many stories of heroic yet not always successful quests, journeys, struggles, and searches.

Without question, the greatest quest is seeking God. People have sought God for various reasons and in many ways. As we'll see, four approaches are woven throughout the Bible.

Lord, You want courageous men to seek and call on You in keeping with Your instructions in Your Word. Yes, Lord, I want to do the same.

REASONS AND WAYS TO SEEK GOD, PART 2

"Yet give attention to your servant's prayer and his plea
for mercy, LORD my God. Hear the cry and the prayer
that your servant is praying in your presence this day."

1 KINGS 8:28

This first approach to seeking God has appealed to mankind
around the world and down through the ages.

1. Men have sought God by praying. The Bible says that
people started to pray to God after Adam and Eve's grandson
Enosh was born (Genesis 4:26). This doesn't mean God stopped
talking directly to individuals. Scripture certainly doesn't tell us
about every instance when He did! Still, God's speaking to man
appears to have tapered off so much that people began initiat-
ing conversations with God through prayer.

Anyone can pray to God—or at least attempt to do so. And
people can pray with all kinds of motives. Many examples of
prayer fill the pages of scripture—some very positive, some very
negative, and some very surprising.

---

*Lord, You want courageous men to seek You through prayer.
I'm so glad I can pray to You anywhere, anytime.*

REASONS AND WAYS TO SEEK GOD, PART 3

I appeal to you therefore, brothers, by the mercies of God,
to present your bodies as a living sacrifice, holy and
acceptable to God, which is your spiritual worship.

ROMANS 12:1 ESV

This second approach to seeking God has been practiced extensively by thousands of people groups, but it hasn't been prevalent in Western countries in recent centuries.

2. Men have sought God by offering sacrifices. Just as the Lord initiated numerous conversations with Adam and Eve, so the Lord initiated the first religious sacrifice after the fall. We can assume the couple started offering sacrifices themselves, just as their sons Cain and Abel did years later. After the flood, Noah offered many sacrifices of thanksgiving to the Lord (Genesis 8:20), eliciting His approval and promises (Genesis 8:21–22). And Moses' instructions from God to His people included sacrifices.

Christians today don't sacrifice animals because Christ became the ultimate sacrifice on the cross. But we do offer our bodies as living sacrifices to God. We give ourselves wholly to Him as an act of worship.

---

*Lord, You want courageous men to be living
sacrifices. May I live according to Your good will
and purposes for my life. Use me for Your glory.*

REASONS AND WAYS TO SEEK GOD, PART 4

"They built high places for Baal in the Valley of Ben Hinnom to sacrifice their sons and daughters to Molek."

JEREMIAH 32:35

I wish I could skip this approach to seeking God, but we have to be true to scripture.

3. *Men have sought God by terrible means.* We find the first huge example only a few pages into the Bible. And by huge, I'm talking the Tower of Babel. Check out Genesis 11:1–9 for the whole story. Did the people really think they could reach into heaven? Talk about a desperate attempt to defy their Maker and disobey His mandate to fill the earth. The Lord laughed, their common language evaporated, and their unfinished tower was abandoned.

You would think such a disaster would make people think twice before seeking God by terrible means, but things only got worse. Much worse: The pantheon of false gods worshipped by the Egyptians. The plethora of false gods worshipped by rebellious Israelites in Egypt, in the wilderness, and then in the Promised Land. Some of this ungodly worship even demanded human sacrifices, especially of children.

Thankfully, God has given us a different way to seek Him. . . .

Lord, You want courageous men to abhor the worship of false gods. I'm repulsed by such things.

REASONS AND WAYS TO SEEK GOD, PART 5

We do this by keeping our eyes on Jesus, the champion who
initiates and perfects our faith. Because of the joy awaiting
him, he endured the cross, disregarding its shame. Now he is
seated in the place of honor beside God's throne.

HEBREWS 12:2 NLT

I've saved the best approach to seeking God for last.

4. Men have sought God by means of the cross. Everything
from Genesis to Malachi points to God's Son, Jesus Christ.
Hundreds of prophecies point to His birth, His earthly ministry,
His sacrificial death on a cross, His physical resurrection from
the dead, and His bodily return to heaven.

True, some anti-Christian skeptics have ridiculed the idea
that God the Father would sacrifice His Son. What's horrific,
however, is that puny human beings would viciously pummel,
beat, flog, and ultimately crucify the perfect, sinless Son of
God. Yes, if Jesus had but said the word, the angels of heaven
could have obliterated these men instantly. Instead, God's Son
willingly and deliberately fulfilled God's rescue plan agreed
upon from eternity past.

The greatest quest is seeking God. Have you found that to
be true yet in your own life and experience?

---

*Lord, You want courageous men to boast
in the cross. I will boast about it today.*

WHAT A SAVIOR

This grace. . .has now been revealed through the appearing
of our Savior, Christ Jesus, who has destroyed death and has
brought life and immortality to light through the gospel.

2 Timothy 1:9-10

During His public ministry here on earth, Jesus saw tens of
thousands of men, women, youth, and children. He saw them
with gracious, loving eyes. He still does.

Jesus wasn't a hypocrite. He didn't just *say* to walk a second mile. He had done it. Maybe more than once. Jesus didn't
just say to turn the other cheek. He had been slapped. Hard.
Jesus didn't just say to give your shirt. When sued, He gave the
man His coat as well.

And there's more. On the day of His death, Jesus, already
severely flogged, walked up the hill to His place of crucifixion.
There, was disrobed, nailed to a cross, lifted up, and
left hanging between heaven and earth while Roman soldiers
divided up all His clothes.

Today, Jesus walks with us, every mile. When we fail Him,
Jesus forgives us and turns the other cheek. Yes, He always
knows we will fail Him again. Still He clothes us with His own
robes of righteousness. And that is how the Lord God sees us,
right now, no matter what. What a Savior!

---

*Lord, You want courageous men to worship Jesus as
their Savior. I gladly worship Jesus as my Savior!*

BEGIN WITH THE END IN MIND

> After that, we who are still alive and are left will be
> caught up together with them in the clouds to meet the
> Lord in the air. And so we will be with the Lord forever.
>
> 1 THESSALONIANS 4:17

Thomas à Kempis's book *The Imitation of Christ* speaks of the importance of beginning with the end in mind. That is, think deeply and often when alone about the day of your death.

I've found it helpful to meditate on Kempis's question, "How do you want to meet God?" To do this—not once, but as a habit of life—creates a sense of excitement and mission about all that we do. Our thoughts, feelings, energy, and choices matter.

Yet how many never give serious thought to the end of their life? Oh, they think they do so—they give thought, often excessively, to the way they would like to finish their years in blissful retirement. *Then*, they tell themselves, *I'll do what I really want. . . .*

But why wait until the end of life to live fully? Why not begin today to give our days completely to God and with eternity in mind?

---

*Lord, You want courageous men to plan, prepare, and
live out their days doing what pleases You. You know my
daydreams. I give them up to do Your will wholeheartedly.*

LIVE ON MISSION

And we urge you, brothers, admonish the idle, encourage
the fainthearted, help the weak, be patient with them all.

1 Thessalonians 5:14 esv

One woman, whose husband's health was failing rapidly,
lamented to Renée and me: "He promised we'd travel the world
together after he retired. We've taken only one trip, and now
he can hardly walk." Her sorrow over all that might have been
shook me.

Ever since, I've made no apology of spending time with
my wife and traveling, a day here, a week there, ever planning
(not just dreaming) of traveling together again. Thanks to grand-
children scattered over the Western United States and Can-
ada, we probably won't traverse the whole planet before my
health is gone, but my wife won't be able to say we didn't try
throughout our life, not just at the end.

The same goes for other dreams, goals, desires. . .if they're
part of our mission, our life's adventures, I see no reason to
wait to go after them, heart and soul.

Pity the person who never decides to live, who never dares
to passionately pursue his plans now—today, this year, the next
five years—before it's too late and our family and friends lament
what might have been.

*Lord, You want courageous men to live out their
mission, their life's adventures. I pledge to do that.*

107

WHEN IT COMES TIME TO DIE

I think it is right to refresh your memory as long as I live in
the tent of this body, because I know that I will soon put it
aside, as our Lord Jesus Christ has made clear to me.

2 PETER 1:13-14

One of the greatest temptations we will ever face in this life is
to spiritually drift away from the Lord. No one is immune—no
matter how long and faithfully they have walked with the Lord.

Thankfully, some wonderful pastors, professors, and men-
tors have helped motivate me to stay in the race until the end.
Probably none influenced me more than Dr. John G. Mitchell.
Never have I met a man who was more in love with the Savior.

On two occasions Dr. Mitchell made a point of reminding
me—more than sixty years his junior—that there are only three
reasons Christians die. These reasons are true in scripture,
in church history, and in our experience today. Believers die
because of the discipline of God (1 Corinthians 11:29-30;
1 John 5:16), for the glory of God (John 21:18-19), or because
their work is finished (2 Timothy 4:6-8).

Dr. Mitchell urged me to make sure, when it comes time to
die, that dying is all I have left to do.

---

*Lord, You want courageous men to finish the
work You assigned to them. Give me a bigger
vision of what You have assigned to me.*

GOD'S BLESSINGS ON OUR LIFE'S WORK

For I am already being poured out like a drink
offering, and the time for my departure is near.

2 TIMOTHY 4:6

The late Dr. Joe Aldrich, former president of what's now Mult-nomah University, is another godly man who motivated me to stay in the Christian race until the end.

On Dr. Joe's desk was the following statement: "I surrender my life into the hands of God, knowing He has predestined for me His best. I will count the cost and by God's grace I will pay the price to become the best that I am capable of becoming. I will hold to my course and by the power of the Holy Spirit, I will finish strong." Powerful words from an amazing man whose ministry and life were cut short by Parkinson's disease.

God allows us to go through deeply troubling, faith-testing periods that can last for weeks, months, years, even decades. The question is always the same: *Will we remain true to God no matter what?*

Through my intensive study of scripture, church history, and contemporary biography, I have become convinced that if we *persevere*, God does something remarkable. He blesses our life's work and impact to an extent we never could have imagined.

Lord, You want courageous men to persevere
in the work You have assigned to them.
I too want to be steadfast until the end.

DON'T STOP BELIEVING GOD'S WORD

Teach me, LORD, the way of your decrees, that I may
follow it to the end. Give me understanding, so that
I may keep your law and obey it with all my heart.

PSALM 119:33–34

Thanks to the influence of cherished men and women in my life,
I love God's Word. I've memorized pages of scripture and read
through the Bible dozens of times. And I've discovered the only
chapters that don't talk about sin and temptation are the first
two and the last two.

From Genesis to Revelation we find that the biggest temptation for believers is to "lose" our faith. How? We stop doing
what the Lord says. Why? We stop believing what God's Word
says.

Think about it. What happened to mighty Judge Samson?
What happened to powerful King Saul? What happened to
wise King Solomon? They all fell away. What about these good
kings—Asa, Joash, Amaziah, Uzziah, and Hezekiah? They followed God for a number of years, then each one turned away.
They didn't lose their final reward, but they lost God's blessings
for staying true to Him until the end.

Not everyone loses faith. But *everyone* will face crises of
life and faith. These pivotal times are part of each person's spiritual journey, yours and mine.

---

*Lord, You want courageous men to acknowledge
temptation. I confess I find it hard to believe that I
could walk away from You, but I'm not immune.*

WE'RE ALL VULNERABLE

I have fought the good fight, I have
finished the race, I have kept the faith.

2 TIMOTHY 4:7

Like Paul, I want to come to the end of my life and say the
words above. That ending isn't a given though. Far from it.

What is the single greatest warning in the Gospels and
Acts? In the New Testament letters from Romans to Jude? Even
in the book of Revelation? Keep following the Lord—endure to
the end—don't fall away.

For many years I thought these biblical warnings didn't
apply to me. Then I was hit with a rapid-fire series of crises:
emergency surgery for my oldest daughter, unexpected house
repairs, two vehicle breakdowns, and a stack of unpaid bills. I
felt that the hand of God was crushing me in every way. In my
despair—and I say this with deep trepidation—I started doubting God's character. I couldn't read the Bible, not a single verse.
I couldn't pray, even over a meal.

I was in danger of losing my faith. Why? Because I'd failed
to heed the clear warnings of scripture. I'd let my circumstances temporarily overshadow what I *knew* to be true. Thank
God for turning me around!

---

*Lord, You want courageous men to turn
around when they stray from Your ways.
Bring me back to You and Your Word.*

LOVE NO MATTER WHAT, PART 1

The goal of this command is love, which comes
from a pure heart and a good conscience and a
sincere faith. Some have departed from these.

1 TIMOTHY 1:5-6

Have you ever winced when you learned that a longtime friend
has left your church? Even harder, did your friend appear to
doubt much of what he used to believe about God, the Bible,
Jesus Christ, the Church, and the Christian faith?

Over the years, after making almost every mistake in the
book, I've discovered and enjoyed using ten counterintuitive
yet powerful steps to follow in a situation like I've described,
and I've seen amazing, God-blessed results. I pray that's your
experience too! Here are the first three:

1. Love your friend unconditionally.

2. Invite your friend to tell his story. When he does, just listen. Don't ask questions. Don't interrupt at all, except to quickly
affirm that you're listening.

3. Be unshockable. Remember, we've all gone astray (Isaiah
53:6). Confession is good for the soul, so let your friend talk.
Don't react to anything he says, no matter how ugly or angry.
He's not angry at you, even if it sounds that way.

---

*Lord, You want courageous men to reach out to those
who walk away. I will reach out to _____ today.*

LOVE NO MATTER WHAT, PART 2

Timothy, guard what has been entrusted to your care.
Turn away from godless chatter and the opposing ideas
of what is falsely called knowledge, which some have
professed and in so doing have departed from the faith.

1 TIMOTHY 6:20–21

Here are the next two counterintuitive ways to love someone who is struggling or has lost his faith.

4. After your friend has finished talking, remain quiet. Keep listening. While on business in Orlando, I met a man named Leonard who poured out his heart to me. I didn't say a word. I just kept listening intently. When he was done, I kept looking into Leonard's angry, deeply hurt eyes and didn't say anything. After a minute, with deepest sadness he said, "All I needed was hope and mercy." What a profoundly haunting lament. Yet if I had started talking, I never would have heard what he needed.

5. Once your friend tells you what he needs, still don't say anything. After Leonard told me, "All I needed was hope and mercy," I remained quiet for another minute. I let my eyes do all the talking. His eyes and facial expressions began to soften and change. Only God's love can do that. Then Leonard told me, "And by listening to my story, you've given me both."

*Lord, You want courageous men to listen,
listen, listen. I will listen to _____.*

LOVE NO MATTER WHAT, PART 3

Their teaching will spread like gangrene. Among them
are Hymenaeus and Philetus, who have departed from
the truth. They say that the resurrection has already
taken place, and they destroy the faith of some.

2 TIMOTHY 2:17–18

Here are two more counterintuitive ways to love someone who is struggling or has lost his faith.

6. Whatever you do, don't promise to meet your friend's needs. Often he wants to know the answer to his burning question, "Why?" You don't know. Don't even try to guess. Speculation will only ruin your credibility.

7. If you and your friend have a mutual friend who has a strong faith in Jesus Christ, explore the possibility of inviting that friend to join you at some point in the future. It's often helpful for people to share their story with a second person. That mutual friend may be a pastor, a professor, a psychologist, or another respected Christian leader. Or that mutual friend may be an "ordinary" but wise individual you both know you can trust.

Lord, You want courageous men to come alongside others while listening to Your leading by Your Spirit. Please lead me as I come alongside _____.

LOVE NO MATTER WHAT, PART 4

Do your best to come to me quickly, for Demas,
because he loved this world, has deserted
me and has gone to Thessalonica.

2 TIMOTHY 4:9-10

Here are the last three counterintuitive ways to love someone who is struggling or has lost his faith.

8. Ask your friend if you can pray for him. If he's in agreement, pray right then. Then remind him from time to time that you're still praying for him. Prayer invites Jesus back into the picture.

9. When your friend is ready, invite him to read the Bible with you. Read one of the four Gospels together. As you read, pray that your friend will fall in love with Jesus again.

10. Stay in touch with your friend no matter what. Your friendship can't be contingent on whether your friend comes back to faith in Jesus Christ. That's up to Him, not you. You may have to hang in there for years before your friend re-embraces faith.

Whatever happens, never give up on your friendship. True, some will walk away. But never let it be said that *you* walked away.

---

*Lord, You want courageous men to come
alongside others for the long haul. I confess that
I feel like giving up on _____, but I won't.*

LOVING THE WHOLE CHURCH

And he [Jesus Christ] is the head of the body, the church;
he is the beginning and the firstborn from among the dead,
so that in everything he might have the supremacy.

COLOSSIANS 1:18

When I talk heart-to-heart with many Christians, I hear a longing to be connected to the whole Church.

There's a growing recognition that the historic branches of the Church share what Rex Koivisto, PhD, author of *One Lord, One Faith*, calls "the core of orthodoxy." That core was intensely forged and mainly consists of a reiteration of the core Gospel truths espoused by Jesus Christ and His apostles. Each branch of Christianity down through the centuries and around the world has borne witness to these truths.

We have much to learn from each of the branches of historic Christianity. Not because these branches offer something new or different, but because they have so many areas of strength. When we draw from the best of the Church, it's marvelous.

---

*Lord, You want courageous men to be church
men, not lone rangers. Thank You for my church.
How do You want me to best serve there?*

FACING TOUGH QUESTIONS

The apostles and elders met
to consider this question.

ACTS 15:6

Here's a weighty question worth raising: *Do my questions have any bearing on the core of orthodoxy?* No. By definition, these core Gospel truths were lived out by Jesus and written out by His apostles nearly two thousand years ago, and their truthfulness remains fixed.

For this reason, I should not be afraid to ask questions. Tough questions. Skeptical questions. Doubting questions. Even angry questions. The very kinds of questions that King David asked some three thousand years ago, fully confident that God was pleased to hear his psalms. All of his psalms. Even the ones we'd rather skip reading.

And for this same reason and more, I also should not be afraid to hear the questions of others. Questions from fellow believers, from struggling saints, from doubters, from skeptics, from agnostics, and even from atheists. Why? Because their questions—even the ones that shock, shake, and stump me—cannot damage, diminish, or disturb the core of orthodox Christianity.

Lord, You want men to courageously face the toughest questions without flinching. I struggle with questions about _____. Strengthen my faith.

HOW LARGE IS TOO LARGE? PART 1

Have you not known? Have you not heard? The LORD
is the everlasting God, the Creator of the ends of
the earth. He does not faint or grow weary;
his understanding is unsearchable.

ISAIAH 40:28 ESV

God's greatness is infinite.

Here on earth, however, "longest" and "heaviest" keep changing.

In 1907, the longest complete dinosaur on record was an eighty-nine-foot-long *Diplodocus* discovered in Wyoming and displayed in Pittsburgh's Carnegie Natural History Museum. Over the past century, much larger beasts have been unearthed around the world. The new heavyweight champions were discovered in Argentina. Like the *Diplodocus*, the fossil records are nearly complete. *Argentinosaurus huinculensis* is an astounding 130 feet long and is estimated to have weighed 96.4 metric tons.

Much larger discoveries could be ahead. And new technologies may speed their discovery. I keep wondering, *At what point will the public in general, and Christians in particular, reach the point of incredulity?*

What happens when the scientific community announces the discovery of a dinosaur whose jaw is large enough to snap *Argentinosaurus* in two? The problem isn't what the Bible teaches. God very well could have created beasts twenty times larger than we've discovered to date. What we need to do now is stretch our God-given imagination.

---

*Lord, You want courageous men to praise Your greatness.
You spoke—and created the whole universe!*

HOW LARGE IS TOO LARGE?
PART 2

Lift up your eyes on high and see: who created these?
He who brings out their host by number, calling them
all by name; by the greatness of his might and because
he is strong in power, not one is missing.

ISAIAH 40:26 ESV

How do we stretch our God-given imagination?

1. Let's indulge in plenty of good humor. Blaise Pascal said: "Nothing produces laughter more than a surprising disproportion between that which one expects and that which one sees." Indeed!

2. Let's continually cultivate humility. When new scientific announcements are made, why not say, "Who knew? Isn't this fascinating? I can't wait to learn more." As well, we may want to add, "Imagine what we might discover in a few more years."

3. Let's pay attention to trends. The changing size of the largest known dinosaurs is one thing. The measurable size of the universe is another. True, I may not reach the point of incredulity (Isaiah 40:27), but I can't assume the same goes for those I know and love.

4. Let's remember that these trends aren't threats to God, Jesus Christ, the Bible, Christianity, or the Church. Instead, let's keep reaffirming that nothing—absolutely nothing—is too big for God to create.

Lord, You want courageous men to praise Your infinite greatness. The universe is nothing compared to You.

IS THERE LIFE OUT THERE?
PART 1

> When I consider your heavens, the work of your
> fingers, the moon and the stars, which you have set
> in place, what is mankind that you are mindful of
> them, human beings that you care for them?
>
> PSALM 8:3–4

Arthur C. Clarke, author of *2001: A Space Odyssey*, once said: "Two possibilities exist: either we are alone in the universe or we are not. Both are equally terrifying."

In 1966, Carl Sagan and Iosef Shklovskii estimated that 0.001 percent of all known stars might have planets capable of sustaining advanced life forms. They made this estimate by extrapolating the likelihood that two variables (the right kind of star with a planet exactly the right distance away) might be repeated elsewhere in the universe.

In 1996, the media had a heyday speculating whether extraterrestrial life may indeed exist, either on Mars or on planets around 47 Ursa Major, 51 Pegasi, 70 Virginis, and other stars. More planets were discovered in 1996 than in the past two millennia. By then, however, the necessary variables had multiplied greatly, to more than forty.

To be continued. . .

Lord, You want men to face the future courageously.
May I never fear the hypothetical.

IS THERE LIFE OUT THERE?
PART 2

*"Where were you when I laid the earth's foundation?
. . . On what were its footings set, or who laid its
cornerstone—while the morning stars sang together
and all the angels shouted for joy?"*

JOB 38:4, 6–7

Fast-forward twenty years from 1996 to 2016. Scientists and reporters alike speculated whether life may exist on a planet circling Proxima Centauri. Traveling at the fantastic velocity of 1.1 million miles an hour, one six-hundredth of the speed of light, it would take nearly five thousand years to travel to Proxima Centauri.

Now fast-forward to today, and the question remains, Is it safe to conclude that life is out there?

Scripture is emphatic: yes, most definitely. God is out there—and here. Celestial beings, good and evil, are out there—and here. And for well over a century, Christian writers such as George MacDonald, C. S. Lewis, Billy Graham, and others have welcomed the idea that other mortal forms of extraterrestrial life may exist.

God is God, so of course it is conceivable and possible. It is no threat to classic Christian belief. Nowhere does the Bible say God created life on this planet alone.

---

*Lord, You want courageous men to embrace
the unknown. May I always trust Your heart.*

FIELDING QUESTIONS AT UC BERKELEY, PART 1

So then, just as you received Christ Jesus as Lord,
continue to live your lives in him, rooted and built
up in him, strengthened in the faith as you were
taught, and overflowing with thankfulness.

COLOSSIANS 2:6–7

Right before I spoke at the University of California Berkeley, organizers issued three distinct warnings. The third warning was that the Free Speech Movement was dead. Any attempt to engage the students in a discussion during my seventy-five-minute presentation would be met with hostility, a walkout, or absolute silence.

Instead, two dozen hands immediately shot up when I asked my first question.

That first question was, "What do UC Berkeley professors say in class that makes it hard to be a Christian?"

One student quoted a professor saying that "Christians are too judgmental." I had to laugh. That very statement is "too judgmental," in my opinion. It appeared that many of the students felt the same way, even though only a handful would have identified themselves as committed followers of Jesus Christ.

---

*Lord, You want men to go anywhere courageously.
Where do You want me to go in coming days?*

FIELDING QUESTIONS AT UC BERKELEY, PART 2

> Greet Andronicus and Junia, my fellow Jews who have
> been in prison with me. They are outstanding among
> the apostles, and they were in Christ before I was.
>
> ROMANS 16:7

I called on a student to my far right. She spoke up for the whole audience to hear. She echoed a women's studies professor's statement that "Christianity has oppressed women."

I tried to be very careful in my response. I like to smile, just not in that moment.

First, I thanked the student for raising this issue and acknowledged I wasn't smart enough to answer it.

Second, I cited three books I helped get published that address this accusation biblically, theologically, and practically. The three books are *Designer Women* by Ruth Tuttle Conard, *Man and Woman, One in Christ* by Philip B. Payne, and *Shepherding Women in Pain* by Bev Hislop.

Third, I acknowledged that some Christians and many more so-called Christians have suppressed and oppressed women throughout the past two millennia. Then again, Jesus Christ and biblical Christianity in the first century and in the twenty-first century have elevated women far above the norms.

In other words, this is a real accusation with real answers.

---

*Lord, You want courageous men to speak the truth
forthrightly and in love. Make me more bold.*

FIELDING QUESTIONS AT UC BERKELEY, PART 3

Where is the wise person? Where is the teacher of the law?
Where is the philosopher of this age? Has not God made
foolish the wisdom of the world?

1 CORINTHIANS 1:20

Maybe twenty-five minutes later I called on a student in the middle of the crowd about two-thirds of the way back. He and three or four of his friends got ready for a good laugh. He said, "Christians are a bunch of hypocrites."

I smiled. "Yes."

Awkward silence, and then a roomful of laughter.

I smiled again. "Yes, you're right. Every Christian I know is a hypocrite. None of us lives up to our ideals. That includes my friends who are Muslim, Jewish, Hindu, Buddhist, or whatever.

"But I would never think of saying to my Buddhist friend that, because he openly admits he doesn't live up to his Buddhist ideals, I don't want to be his friend anymore. To me, that's unthinkable.

"So, yes, you're right, all Christians are hypocrites."

*Lord, You want courageous men to admit
they aren't perfect. Thank You for Your
marvelous, amazing mercy and grace.*

FIELDING QUESTIONS AT UC BERKELEY, PART 4

See to it that no one takes you captive through
hollow and deceptive philosophy, which depends
on human tradition and the elemental spiritual
forces of this world rather than on Christ.

COLOSSIANS 2:8

I went one by one until each student who wanted to do so gave an answer to my question, "What do UC Berkeley professors say in class that makes it hard to be a Christian?"

I was shocked that I had heard all their answers when I was in college. In other words, the professors hadn't taught the students any new accusations in decades. As if "Christians are a bunch of hypocrites" really is the best they can do. Astounding!

Would I walk back onto the campus of UC Berkeley to speak again? In a heartbeat.

Then again, the reality is many followers of Jesus Christ walk onto the Berkeley campus every day. As staff. As students. And, yes, as professors. Those I know are amazing individuals who have my highest regard.

Imagine stepping into their shoes right now.

If you feel so led, please keep them and their fellow believers in every university in your prayers.

Lord, You want courageous men to pray against strongholds. Please bring revival to our universities.

HOW JESUS AND PAUL
RESPECTED WOMEN

Greet Priscilla and Aquila, my co-workers in Christ Jesus.
They risked their lives for me. Not only I but all the
churches of the Gentiles are grateful to them.

ROMANS 16:3–4

Sadly, you don't have to go to UC Berkeley to meet people who believe "Christianity has oppressed women." Without question, certain religious people and groups have horribly oppressed women over the years. But let's never make the categorical error of equating those terrible oppressors with true Christianity, with the Christianity of Jesus Christ and His apostles.

That error, however, has become pervasive in the past generation. We hear it in statements like: "Paul hated women" or "Christianity started with an egalitarian view of gender relations taught by Jesus, but this was destroyed by Paul."

The facts? Jesus and the apostle Paul lived in a world dominated by the severely oppressive religious views of that century's Jewish rabbis. But in a careful review of the twelve malicious ways the ancient rabbis oppressed women, we find both Jesus and Paul doing the exact opposite at every point.

In thought, word, and deed, Jesus always loved, respected, and honored women—and so did Paul. This is impossible to miss in Romans 16, where the apostle applauds ten women within fifteen verses.

Lord, You want courageous men to applaud courageous women of God. I want to honor _____ .

THE GOOD HUSBAND, PART 1

A wife of noble character who can find?
She is worth far more than rubies.

PROVERBS 31:10

Behind every successful man, the saying goes, there's a good woman. And that's often the case. But have you ever considered that behind many successful women, there's a good man?

That is the message of Proverbs 31. Only the Lord Himself knows how many articles and sermons, books and seminars have extolled the virtues of the Wonder Woman described in this poetic passage. The only problem is they have usually forgotten to mention the *other* main character—the Good Husband!

Was Proverbs 31 ever intended to be an idealistic standard for women to attain by themselves? Not at all. Instead, this passage of scripture, like the rest of Proverbs, was written originally as a challenge to *men*.

It's all too easy for guys to read Proverbs 31:10–31 rather flippantly—"Wow, if only I had a wife like this!"—without stopping to notice what these verses say about this woman's rather remarkable husband.

Lord, You want courageous men to
learn from Proverbs 31. I'm ready!

THE GOOD HUSBAND, PART 2

Her husband has full confidence in her and lacks nothing of value. She brings him good, not harm, all the days of her life.

PROVERBS 31:11-12

What does Proverbs 31 say about the Good Husband?

1. He cherishes his wife. The Good Husband recognizes the true value of his wife as a person. He sees her as God's price-less, one of a kind masterpiece. He knows she's "worth far more than rubies" (verse 10).

The world says you're worth something only if you're beautiful, intelligent, or athletic. But that isn't God's measure of true value. Self-worth isn't based on what you do, but who you are—a person created in the image of God.

Richard Strauss reminds us that when a woman is loved for who she is, she "will blossom into the most beautiful creature under God's heaven."

A man beautifies his wife by cherishing her for who she is. He doesn't let his wife lose her sense of specialness once the honeymoon is over. He continues to court her. With his words, touches, and actions a husband lets his wife know she is the most important person in his life.

Lord, You want courageous husbands to cherish their wives. Teach all of us as men—whether married or not—what cherishing means.

THE GOOD HUSBAND, PART 3

She considers a field and buys it; out of her earnings she plants a vineyard. She sets about her work vigorously; her arms are strong for her tasks. She sees that her trading is profitable, and her lamp does not go out at night.

PROVERBS 31:16–18

What else does Proverbs 31 say about the Good Husband?

2. He supports his wife. The Good Husband believes in the potential of his wife (verse 11). He doesn't put her in a box called "home." Instead, he allows her to be productive and fulfilled both in and out of the home.

Frankly, the Good Husband of Proverbs 31 amazes me. How many husbands are willing to let their wives make real estate investments and start business ventures on their own? How many husbands are willing to let their wives make contributions to charitable organizations as they see fit (verse 20)? Traditionally in our society, the husband has been viewed as solely responsible for the family income and budget. But the Good Husband challenges these cultural norms.

The biblical concept of submission encompasses the idea of assuming a supportive role. Both men and women are called to "submit to one another" (Ephesians 5:21). The Good Husband actively supports his wife as she seeks to reach her full potential as a person.

Lord, You want courageous husbands to support their wives. Show me how to be a supportive man.

THE GOOD HUSBAND, PART 4

She opens her arms to the poor and extends her
hands to the needy. When it snows, she has no fear
for her household; for all of them are clothed in scarlet.

PROVERBS 31:20–21

Reread the last sentence of yesterday's devotion. Did you catch an important word? The Good Husband *actively* supports his wife as she seeks to reach her full potential as a person.

Anne Morrow once wrote: "Ideally, both members of a couple in love free each other to new and different worlds. I was no exception. . . . The man I was to marry believed in me and what I could do, and consequently I found I could do more than I ever realized." With her husband's encouragement, she became one of America's most popular authors.

One of the greatest forces for growth and change in our lives is someone who believes in us. The mark of marital maturity is the ability to help your spouse achieve and succeed. The Good Husband is mature enough to encourage and support his wife to reach her full potential.

He believes in her and provides an atmosphere in which she is free to succeed. He doesn't let his ego get in her way.

---

*Lord, You want courageous husbands to
open doors for their wives. Show me
what opening doors looks like.*

THE GOOD HUSBAND, PART 5

She is clothed with strength and dignity; she can
laugh at the days to come. She speaks with wisdom,
and faithful instruction is on her tongue.

PROVERBS 31:25–26

What's the next thing Proverbs 31 says about the Good Husband?

3. *He listens to his wife.* The Good Husband realizes the importance of listening to the wisdom of his wife. He is spared from many rash and foolish actions by respecting the "faithful instruction. . .on her tongue" (verse 26).

Pilate was warned by his wife not to harm the Lord Jesus Christ (Matthew 27:19). Yet he chose to ignore her wise counsel and had the Son of God crucified instead. The Good Husband is careful not to repeat Pilate's folly.

I enjoy actively listening to my wife. She has taught me much about God and about life. No, I haven't relinquished my responsibility as the spiritual leader in our home. But we enjoy mutually stimulating one another spiritually and intellectually. No day is complete unless we have an opportunity to share new insights with each other. I'm never the loser when I give Renée my undivided attention as she shares with me.

---

*Lord, You want courageous husbands to listen to
their wives. Teach me to be a good listener.*

THE GOOD HUSBAND, PART 6

She watches over the affairs of her household and does not
eat the bread of idleness. Her children arise and call her
blessed; her husband also, and he praises her.

PROVERBS 31:27–28

Again, the Good Husband strengthens his marriage by taking
the time to listen to his wife. He respects her opinions and
heeds her advice.

Hudson Taylor is credited with starting the China Inland
Mission, one of the most successful groups to penetrate China
with the Gospel before World War II. But the secret of Taylor's
success was a wife who poured every fiber of her being into
him and their work. Taylor leaned heavily on his wife, Maria,
for wisdom and strength in those early pioneering days. Biogra-
phers say he never took a step without consulting her.

Why are so many couples failing in their marriages? How-
ard Hendricks gave this answer: "They have taken no time to
cultivate their own relationship, [and] listen to each other."
Imagine what God could do through a couple committed to
listening to—and learning from—each other.

---

*Lord, You want courageous husbands to learn
from their wives. Make me open to learning.*

THE GOOD HUSBAND, PART 7

Her husband. . .praises her: "Many women do noble things,
but you surpass them all." Charm is deceptive, and
beauty is fleeting; but a woman who fears the LORD is to
be praised. Honor her for all that her hands have done,
and let her works bring her praise at the city gate.

PROVERBS 31:28–31

What's the last thing that Proverbs 31 says about the Good Husband?

4. He praises his wife. The Good Husband praises the virtues and accomplishments of his wife. He doesn't flatter her, but praises his wife for her fear of God and her successful endeavors. He lets others know that his wife is extra special. It means much to a woman to know her husband speaks highly of her to others.

A man can never praise, compliment, or build up his wife too much. Everyone craves appreciation, and wives perhaps need (and deserve!) it the most. A husband can make a tremendous impact on his wife by consciously and consistently telling her what he appreciates about her. There are few transforming forces more powerful than loving praise.

One final thought: The Good Husband doesn't expect his wife to automatically duplicate the virtues of the Wonder Woman described so poetically in Proverbs 31. Instead, he encourages his wife, and she does the same for him!

---

*Lord, You want courageous husbands to praise
their wives. Train me to be a man of praise.*

WRESTLING WITH THREE PROBING QUESTIONS, PART 1

> Love the LORD your God with all your heart and
> with all your soul and with all your strength.
>
> DEUTERONOMY 6:5

I've learned the hard way that every Christian needs the courage to ask three probing questions:

1. Do I understand the greatest commandment and take it seriously?

2. Do I understand that I can love God wholeheartedly *only* if I embrace His deep love for me?

3. Do I understand that I can love my neighbors as myself *only* if I love myself?

Each of these questions hinges on the others. If we don't love ourselves, for instance, then loving others as ourselves is problematic, and the greatest commandment is mere theory.

I spent three days with Jerry and Denise Basel at their home north of Atlanta. Jerry and Denise wrote the book *The Missing Commandment: Love Yourself.* They're the real deal with a powerful message. Together, they resolved a deep, nagging concern in my own life: What does it mean for me to obey Jesus' command to love others "as yourself"?

We'll dig into the answers to these questions in the next few devotions.

---

*Lord, You want courageous men to seek answers
to important questions. I'm ready to learn more.*

WRESTLING WITH THREE PROBING QUESTIONS, PART 2

"Do not seek revenge or bear a grudge
against anyone among your people, but love
your neighbor as yourself. I am the LORD."

LEVITICUS 19:18

Whenever Jesus was asked which commandment is most important, He replied, "Love the Lord your God with all your heart, all your soul, all your strength, and all your mind."

Then He would add, "The second is this: 'Love your neighbor as yourself.' There is no commandment greater than these."

In His first sentence about loving God, Jesus echoed the words of Deuteronomy 6:5. In His second sentence about loving others as ourselves, Jesus quoted Leviticus 19:18.

The supreme priority of these two statements stands out more clearly in Matthew 22:40 when Jesus declared, "All the Law and the Prophets hang on these two commandments."

There is nothing more important in all the scriptures, in terms of what God asks of us, than to love Him wholeheartedly and to love others as we love ourselves.

Lord, You want courageous men to obey the greatest commandment. Help me understand how to do that.

WRESTLING WITH THREE PROBING QUESTIONS, PART 3

> Hearing that Jesus had silenced the Sadducees, the Pharisees got together. One of them, an expert in the law, tested him with this question: "Teacher, which is the greatest commandment in the Law?"
>
> MATTHEW 22:34-36

It's not possible to obey the greatest commandment, however, if we don't embrace God's deep love personally. First John 4:19 says, "We love because he first loved us."

Sadly, many think God does not look on them with love, favor, and delight. In their heart of hearts, they actually feel that God is angry at them or, at best, distant and uncaring. This is the great disconnect that the Father wants to remedy in each one of us.

In her book *Breaking Free*, Beth Moore tells the story of a group of women she was teaching about God's love. She asked them to look into the eyes of the person next to them and say, "God loves *me* so much." Guess what happened all over the room? "The women turned to one another and said, 'God loves *you* so much,'" Moore wrote.

What a perfect example of how we accept God's love for others but struggle to believe in His love for us. Yet the truth is God loves you and me just as much as He loves others. Why do we believe otherwise?

---

*Lord, You want courageous men to embrace
Your love for them. Thank You for loving me!*

WRESTLING WITH THREE PROBING QUESTIONS, PART 4

"Well said, teacher," the man replied. "You are right in saying that God is one and there is no other but him. To love him with all your heart, with all your understanding and with all your strength, and to love your neighbor as yourself is more important than all burnt offerings and sacrifices."

MARK 12:32–33

When we embrace God's deep love for us, we become better able to love others in return. Loving what God loves is the key—and yes, He absolutely loves each of us. In Jeremiah 31:3, the Lord said, "I have loved you with an everlasting love."

One man told his church that he knew in his head that God loved him, but for the very first time he had experienced a profound revelation of "Jesus loves me, this I know" deep within his heart. To say he was transformed by this experience doesn't do it justice.

If learning to embrace God's deep love for *me* changes how I think of myself and ultimately enables me to love *you* better, then the results are decidedly *unselfish*. Experiencing God's love for me in a much deeper way has transformed how I see and treat myself and others.

In coming days, may that be *your* experience—an experience well worth sharing.

Lord, You want courageous men to love
others well. I want to love _____ well today.

PETER'S CALLING AND OURS

The first thing Andrew did was to find his brother Simon and tell him, "We have found the Messiah" (that is, the Christ). And he brought him to Jesus. Jesus looked at him and said, "You are Simon son of John. You will be called Cephas" (which, when translated, is Peter).

JOHN 1:41–42

Have you ever noticed that the apostle Peter's calling didn't happen suddenly? Instead, it occurred progressively over the course of four occasions.

The first occasion is recorded in John 1. Andrew invited his brother to meet Jesus. This was a pivotal experience for Peter, but it was only the start.

The second occasion is recorded in Luke 5. Jesus preached from Peter's boat. Peter was overcome with Jesus' righteousness and his own sinfulness. In many ways, this was Peter's conversion experience.

The third occasion is recorded in Mark 1 and Matthew 4. It followed closely on the heels of the second occasion. Jesus now commanded Andrew and Peter, and their partners James and John, "Follow Me and I will make you fishers of men." When Peter said yes, his calling was confirmed.

The fourth occasion is recorded in Luke 6. Jesus drew all His followers together and appointed Peter as one of His twelve apostles.

Lord, You want courageous men to say "Yes!" to Your calling on their life. Right now, I am saying "Yes!" to You.

JESUS CALLS US TO
HONOR THE HUMBLE

One Sabbath, when Jesus went to eat in the house of a
prominent Pharisee, he was being carefully watched.

LUKE 14:1

The Pharisees had set a trap. They invited Jesus to dinner, and
when He arrived at the house, a man with dropsy was waiting.
Jesus wasted no time turning the tables on them. He ques-
tioned their motives: "Is it lawful to heal on the Sabbath or
not?" (Luke 14:3). Then, He took hold of the man, healed him,
and sent him away.

Jesus proceeded to weave a story with a point: "All those
who exalt themselves will be humbled, and those who humble themselves will be exalted" (Luke 14:11). Jesus rebuked His
host. He told him to stop inviting his family, friends, and digni-
taries. "Instead," Jesus said in effect, "do what you did today.
Invite a man with dropsy. What's more, be sure to invite all
his friends. For when you invite the poor, diseased, crippled,
lame, and blind, you will be blessed by God and handsomely
rewarded at the resurrection of the righteous."

"The humble will be exalted" isn't just in heaven. It's here
on earth, right now. This adds width and depth to Christian
hospitality.

---

*Lord, You want courageous men to practice
radical hospitality. Please identify who
You want me to show hospitality to.*

HONOR OTHERS BY LISTENING TO THEIR STORIES

After three days they found him in the temple
courts, sitting among the teachers, listening
to them and asking them questions.

LUKE 2:46

Hung Thach serves with Cru High School in Long Beach, California. When he first moved there, Hung felt led by the Lord to visit a skate park near Long Beach Polytechnic High School. There he met Jose, Jose's brother Scotty, and their friend Jacob. When Hung asked if they would like to get a bite to eat, all three said yes.

While they were eating, Hung began to give his testimony. Jose began to rock back and forth. This puzzled Hung, so he asked if Jose was bored or wanted to go home. Jose replied, "No, I'm not bored. I was wondering: When can I tell you my story?" Hung immediately asked him, "What's your story?"

When Jose had finished, Hung asked to hear Scotty's and Jacob's stories. All three were filled with family tragedies, death, and poverty.

Hung then had the privilege of sharing the greatest story, about Jesus. That day, Jose and Scotty began a personal relationship with Jesus Christ. Since then, Hung and his team have offered meals, listened to stories, and seen hundreds of Long Beach high school students give their lives to Jesus Christ. May their tribe increase!

*Lord, You want courageous men to ask others
to tell their stories. Show me who to ask.*

HOW JESUS GETS OUR ATTENTION

He said to them, "How foolish you are, and how slow to believe all that the prophets have spoken! Did not the Messiah
have to suffer these things and then enter his glory?" And
beginning with Moses and all the Prophets, he explained to
them what was said in all the Scriptures concerning himself.

LUKE 24:25–27

Near the end of Luke's Gospel, we find a post-resurrection
story about Jesus appearing to Cleopas and a friend on the
road to Emmaus. But His actions aren't what we might expect.

First, Jesus disguised Himself.

Then Jesus played dumb and asked Cleopas why he was
so sad.

Jesus listened to all Cleopas had to say. Cleopas talked
about his belief that Jesus was a prophet, his shattered hopes
that Jesus might have been the Christ, and his confused
thoughts about the empty tomb.

Jesus wasn't ready to reveal Himself yet, but He was
ready to set Cleopas straight! And Jesus didn't come in soft
and sweet. "You fools," Jesus said, in essence. "You slow-
hearted doubters. You're unwilling to connect the dots and
believe what is so clearly revealed throughout the scriptures."

Why did Jesus speak harshly? He did so out of love. And
Jesus did so because harsh words get our *full* attention in a way
nothing else will.

---

*Lord, You want courageous men to listen when You
speak to their hearts—even when it's harsh! Help me listen.*

EMBRACING THE GREAT COMMISSION

"And proclaim as you go, saying,
'The kingdom of heaven is at hand.'"

MATTHEW 10:7 ESV

Each of the first five books of the New Testament clearly state the Great Commission.

In Matthew, Jesus said: "Go and make disciples of all nations, baptizing them in the name of the Father and of the Son and of the Holy Spirit, and teaching them to obey everything I have commanded you" (28:19-20).

In Mark, Jesus said: "Go into all the world and preach the gospel to all creation" (16:15).

In Luke, Jesus said: "This is what is written: The Messiah will suffer and rise from the dead on the third day, and repentance for the forgiveness of sins will be preached in his name to all nations, beginning at Jerusalem" (24:46-47).

In John, Jesus said: "Peace be with you! As the Father has sent me, I am sending you" (20:21).

In Acts, Jesus said: "You will receive power when the Holy Spirit comes on you; and you will be my witnesses in Jerusalem, and in all Judea and Samaria, and to the ends of the earth" (1:8).

Have you accepted the commission?

---

*Lord, You want courageous men to embrace
the Great Commission. I understand that my
"Jerusalem" is right here, right now.*

THE PRODIGAL COMES HOME

"When he came to his senses, he said, '. . .I will set out and go back to my father and say to him: Father, I have sinned against heaven and against you. I am no longer worthy to be called your son; make me like one of your hired servants.'"

LUKE 15:17–19

The first time I read the story of the prodigal son, I had no idea how his Jewish father would respond to his shocking demands. Would he disown his son, order his servants to throw the rebel out of the mansion, and declare him "dead" to the family?

In many cultures around the world, that's what would be expected. The son's high-handed, insulting, and shameful behavior wouldn't be tolerated in any decent society.

Instead, the Jewish father gives the son what he asks for. The rest of the story doesn't make much more sense. No wealthy, respected gentleman would long for such a notorious, shameful son to come back home. And yet. . .he welcomes the prodigal with open arms!

The prodigal's father is a picture of our heavenly Father, who treats us just as astonishingly. Even when we don't believe in God, He believes in us. He hopes for the best. He expects a miracle. And He can't wait to throw a party in our honor.

Lord, when they sin, You want courageous men to turn back to You. I need to do that myself today.

TWO WAYS TO EXPERIENCE DEEP SUFFERING

One of the criminals who hung there hurled insults at
   him: "Aren't you the Messiah? Save yourself and us!"
   But the other criminal rebuked him. "Don't you fear
God," he said, "since you are under the same sentence?"

LUKE 23:39–40

In the two thieves that were crucified next to Jesus, we see two
ways that humanity experiences deep suffering.

Like the first thief, we can feel spite toward Jesus until our
dying breath, choosing the vocabulary and habitations of hell as
our only escape from Him.

Like the second thief, we can choose repentance. That is,
we can turn from our life of sin, call out to Jesus, and receive
rock-solid hope and assurance in our darkest hour.

In between the two thieves, of course, is the cross of our
Lord and Savior, Jesus. The day of Christ's death, supernatural
darkness blanketed that part of the world from noon to three
o'clock. In the scriptures, such darkness represents God's judgment. Here it showed God the Father's judgment on the sins
of the whole world, which Jesus willingly bore in His own body.

I am *not* saying that our deep suffering is an indication of
God's judgment. No, not unless we've consciously committed
some egregious, ongoing sins. Instead, our sufferings are
meant to draw us into our Savior's amazing love and absolute
forgiveness.

Lord, You want courageous men to cry out to You.
Thank You so much for Your salvation.

INTRODUCING OTHERS TO JESUS

Then Nathanael declared, "Rabbi, you are
the Son of God; you are the king of Israel."

JOHN 1:49

Some Jewish religious leaders demanded to know who John the Baptist was. John laughed and said, "Well, for sure I'm not the Christ." The leaders then went down through their predetermined list of possible identities—Are you Elijah? Are you the Prophet?—only for John to say, "No. No. No."

This string of denials frustrated the priests and Levites to no end. "Then who are you?" they demanded. John told them that he was the one who was paving the way for the Lord, *the One*, whose sandals John was not worthy to untie (John 1:23, 27).

The very next day, who walked by? John the Baptist gave Him an ancient, sacred name: "The Lamb of God, who takes away the sin of the world" (John 1:29). He was "God's Chosen One" (John 1:34), the Son of God.

The day after that? John the Baptist was talking with two of his disciples, when he said, "Look, the Lamb of God!" (John 1:36). That introduction was all the men needed to rush to catch up with Jesus. *It completely changed their lives.*

Today, we have the privilege to introduce people to this same Man.

---

*Lord, You want courageous men to introduce others
to Your Son. Today I will speak about Jesus.*

THE WOMAN CAUGHT IN ADULTERY

But Jesus bent down and started to write on the ground
with his finger. When they kept on questioning him,
he straightened up and said to them, "Let any one of you
who is without sin be the first to throw a stone at her."
Again he stooped down and wrote on the ground.

JOHN 8:6–8

Early one morning Jesus walked into the temple and began teaching the people. They listened as He spoke words of truth with authority.

Yet almost immediately a commotion drew their attention. Jewish religious leaders were shouting at a woman who was weeping, wailing, and fighting for her life. This mob of men cared nothing for her. She was a pawn in their latest futile attempt to trap Jesus into saying something they could report to the Roman governor, Pontius Pilate, who alone had the authority to sentence a man to death.

It's almost certain that the unnamed woman really was caught in adultery. It's also likely that the religious leaders orchestrated the rendezvous and then let the man "escape." How convenient. How dastardly. How hypocritical.

But with only a few words, Jesus disgraced His enemies and liberated this woman. She was free. . .forgiven. . .changed. She was loved by the Savior. Her story, down through the ages, has offered hope and healing to millions.

---

*Lord, You want courageous men to share this life-changing
Gospel story with others. I will share it today.*

THE CERTAINTY OF JESUS' RESURRECTION

> "You killed the author of life, but God raised him
> from the dead. We are witnesses of this."
>
> ACTS 3:15

Have you ever wondered why Matthew, Mark, and Luke go to the trouble of revealing the initial doubts and disbelief of the disciples on that first Easter morning? Later that day, Jesus would erase all doubts.

First, Jesus showed them His hands and feet. Imagine His mother walking up, crying, seeing firsthand that the wounds have been replaced by healing scars.

Second, Jesus invited them to touch Him, because "a ghost does not have flesh and bones," but He did (Luke 24:39). Imagine Mary Magdalene taking a step back. Earlier this day Jesus had told her not to keep holding on to His feet. "It's okay, Mary," Jesus now says. "Show them." She smiles, walks forward, kneels, places her hands on His ankles, and kisses His nail-scarred feet.

Third, Jesus asked for some food to eat. He didn't do this because He was hungry. Instead, Jesus wanted to prove beyond a doubt that He wasn't an apparition, a ghost, a spirit being. So, He ate a piece of cooked fish. By now, all doubt was erased. Joy, gladness, and delight overcame the disciples.

---

*Lord, You want courageous men to believe
and proclaim the bodily resurrection of Jesus.
I believe and will speak of it today.*

WAS JESUS PROUD OF THE GOSPEL?

> "This gospel of the kingdom will be preached in
> the whole world as a testimony to all nations."
>
> MATTHEW 24:14

Ready for four important questions?

Number one: Was Jesus Christ ever ashamed of the Gospel message? Of course not. It was the very heartbeat of everything He said, did, and is.

Number two: Was the apostle Paul ever ashamed of the Gospel of Jesus Christ? Again, of course not. Just think about what he wrote to believers in Rome: "I am not ashamed of the gospel, for it is the power of God for salvation to everyone who believes" (Romans 1:16 ESV).

Number three: Was Jesus proud of the Gospel? It's true that pride tops the list of the seven deadly sins that God hates the most. But there is also good pride—pride that God is at work in and through us. So of course, yes, Jesus was and is proud of the Gospel message.

Number four: Was Paul proud of the Gospel? Again, yes of course. "It's news I'm most proud to proclaim, this extraordinary Message," he wrote (Romans 1:16 MSG). "I am proud of the good news!" (Romans 1:16 CEV).

Can we say the same?

---

*Lord, You want courageous men to be proud
of the life-changing Good News of Jesus
Christ. Today, I won't be ashamed.*

ARE YOU PROUD OF THE GOSPEL?

It's news I'm most proud to proclaim, this extraordinary
Message of God's powerful plan to rescue
everyone who trusts him.

ROMANS 1:16 MSG

We'd like to think that we're as proud of the Gospel as Paul was. Then again, when we hem and haw, when we cop out, when we never say anything, people are disappointed. Sometimes, they're outright offended that we are ashamed of the Good News of Jesus Christ.

My friend Kevin Harney, an author and pastor, puts it this way: "People today want to know what we believe—and want to know that we believe it wholeheartedly!"

Another good friend, Kevin Palau, president of the Palau Association, adds: "My hope for every follower of Christ [is] to love our neighbors, not condemn them. To serve those in need, not shy away from them. And to do it all boldly in the name of Jesus Christ."

What about you? Are you proud of the Good News? Are you living your life boldly in the name of Christ? If not, remember the words of Kevin Harney and Kevin Palau. More importantly, remember the words of the apostle Paul.

Lord, You want courageous men to proudly talk
about the Gospel. I will do that today—and every day.

TALKING WITH YOUR NEIGHBORS

If you really keep the royal law found in Scripture,
"Love your neighbor as yourself," you are doing right.

JAMES 2:8

Augustine and Pascal were right: we're restless until we accept God's love, forgiveness, and life. Until then, people are dissatisfied, even if they don't know why. We might see this when we take the time to listen to the life story of a neighbor.

Your neighbor may ask you why God allowed the hardest episodes in their life. Instead of trying to explain "why," you can ask them a question of your own: "Would you be willing to read the story of Jesus and then tell me what you think about it?"

You're not saying, ". . .and then I'll tell you what to believe." You're not leading a Bible study. You're not leading a discussion. You're simply inviting them to read a chapter or two, get together with you again, and tell you what they think about the chapters.

Be sure to say "Jesus," not "Christ." Yes, we're used to saying "Christ." But others aren't used to hearing it, and it often means something different to them than it means to you and me. Our neighbors don't fall in love with "Christ." They fall in love with Jesus.

---

*Lord, You want courageous men to speak
about Your Son to their hurting neighbors.
I will talk with _____ about Jesus.*

HOW SOMEONE BECOMES A CHRISTIAN

"Everyone who calls on the name
of the Lord will be saved."

ROMANS 10:13

Did you know that praying with someone isn't the only way a person can become a Christian?

If God tells you to lead a neighbor, relative, or friend in a prayer of salvation, do so! But the New Testament never says that Jesus used or preferred such an approach.

The same is true of the apostle Paul. Some say, "Wait! What about Romans 10:9–10?" There Paul wrote that "if you declare with your mouth, 'Jesus is Lord,' and believe in your heart that God raised him from the dead, you will be saved. For it is with your heart that you believe and are justified, and it is with your mouth that you profess your faith and are saved."

The plain meaning of these two verses is that someone hears the Gospel message and believes in and professes Jesus as Lord and Savior. Nowhere does either verse hint of a prayer of salvation. And that's true in fifty-three Bible translations.

Lord, You want courageous men to trust Your Spirit at work in people's hearts. I will listen to the testimony of someone without correcting them if they don't say, "I prayed a prayer."

TAILORING OUR APPROACH

The Son is the radiance of God's glory
and the exact representation of his being.

HEBREWS 1:3

What's our mind-set when we talk with neighbors, friends, or acquaintances? It's not enough to hear their story. It's not enough to help them see how their story connects with God's "big story." It's not even enough to get them into the scriptures.

Sometimes, depending on their religious background, we need to tailor our approach. With a Buddhist or Hindu friend, for instance, you don't want to start with Genesis. Instead, go straight to the story of Jesus in the Gospels.

With a couple of Jehovah's Witnesses, ask if you can read the Gospel of John together using their New World Translation. Yes, they've changed the meaning of John 1:1. But most of the NWT is old-fashioned, accurate, and unread by the majority of Jehovah's Witnesses. The very fact that we ask to read *their* Bible with them may surprise them. That we ask questions may surprise them even more.

The biggest surprise, however, is when we keep asking questions with a smile on our face that makes them look at what John's Gospel really says about Jesus Christ.

The Lord isn't nervous when you read other people's scriptures. You don't need to be nervous either.

---

*Lord, You want courageous men to use
all means to win people to Jesus Christ.
What means do You want me to use today?*

LOVING REFUGEES AND IMMIGRANTS

> The angel of the LORD also said to her: "You are now
> pregnant and you will give birth to a son. You shall name
> him Ishmael, for the LORD has heard of your misery."
>
> GENESIS 16:11

What's our mind-set when we talk with refugees and immigrants? Sometimes, depending on their religious culture, we need to tailor our approach.

With some of our friends, we may want to ask if we can read the Koran with them. The Koran is highly revered but largely unread by the majority of people who own a copy.

The very fact that we ask to read *their* scriptures, and then affirm what the Koran says that echoes or agrees with the Christian and Hebrew scriptures, will surprise them.

Often, the bigger surprise for them is discovering that many things the Koran teaches are quite different or even opposite of what they've heard and been taught their whole life.

Then we can ask to read parallel accounts about our common spiritual fathers, including Abraham, the father of the world's three monotheistic religions.

Jesus isn't nervous when you read non-biblical scriptures. You don't need to be either.

---

*Lord, You want courageous men to use all means
to reach those who come here from foreign lands.
Help me reach out to _____.*

LOVING OUR ASIAN NEIGHBORS AND FRIENDS

Sing to the LORD a new song,
his praise from the ends of the earth.

ISAIAH 42:10

Toward the end of a workshop at a large Christian leadership conference in San Francisco, I opened the floor for questions. On my far right sat an Asian American man. He raised his hand and shared a detailed story about loving one of his Japanese neighbors. Years later, he had the joy of hearing his neighbor say he was now a follower of Jesus Christ. The man choked up for a few seconds. Then his face grew serious. "It's hard for me to explain," he said.

I replied: "You didn't tell your neighbor to stop going to his Shinto shrine?"

The man's face lit up. "Yes, yes! I felt God telling me *not* to say anything. God told me that *He* would tell my neighbor later. And about six months later, God did just that. And that, I believe, is the reason why he continues to follow Jesus and now comes with me to my church."

Some have asked, "Why would God wait? Shouldn't the neighbor have quit going to the shrine immediately?"

How good that we can trust the Lord and thank Him daily for His sovereignty and providence, holiness and love, and mystery. May we always acquiesce to Him.

---

*Lord, You want courageous men to trust Your work
in someone's heart. Other religions don't faze You.
Help me reach out to _____.*

LOVING OUR NONRELIGIOUS FRIENDS

For the wages of sin is death, but the gift of
God is eternal life in Christ Jesus our Lord.

ROMANS 6:23

I invite you to read what a young woman named Katie told me. She lives in my hometown of Portland, Oregon, which has an extra-large percentage of nonreligious residents:

"I was raised in a postmodern home. I don't remember from the early years there being a lot of negativity around religion. There was just a void of talking about anything spiritual.

"I remember that one of the biggest hurdles for me was actually the idea of sin. This isn't something that is talked about in non-Christian homes. At least not in mine. We were raised to believe that all people are essentially good, and we all make mistakes but, if given the right tools and resources, we will make good choices.

"Once I was able to wrap my mind around the idea of sin and therefore the need for Jesus, the rest happened pretty quickly. I became a believer that December. I was listening to a CD that my friend Elizabeth had given me for Christmas. I remember having this knowledge that Jesus was pursuing me, that He wanted me to know Him. I also realized that, while I didn't know what it would mean in my life, I wanted Him too."

Lord, You want courageous men to use creative means
to share You with others. How can I do that today?

LOVING OUR ATHEISTIC RELATIVES

In his pride the wicked man does not seek him;
in all his thoughts there is no room for God.

PSALM 10:4

Recently my dad told me, "If I had to believe in something, I probably would believe in Odin" (the god of Norse mythology). My dad is half Norwegian, so it kind of makes sense.

To pay my dues to my dad's disbelief, at age eighteen I studied under a German existential philosopher. She was a happy atheist, and we had a truly wonderful time working our way through more than four centuries of atheistic thought. My challenge to her: "Convert me or I'll probably be a Christian the rest of my life." I had decided to follow Jesus Christ wholeheartedly at age thirteen but deliberately put my faith on the shelf.

In the end, I realized I had an even more robust faith in Jesus. That doesn't make me one bit smarter or better than my dad. Still, I would love to see my dad put his atheism on the shelf awhile and happily study Jesus. I think if he read the Gospels, he very well might fall in love with Jesus. . .just like I did years ago.

---

*Lord, You want courageous men to read the
Gospels with even the most resistant men.
Show me who I can invite into Your Word with me.*

PROMISING TO FINISH WELL

For I am already being poured out like a drink
offering, and the time for my departure is near.

2 TIMOTHY 4:6

A few months before his death, Dr. Ted Engstrom invited me to
spend a day together, just the two of us. His eyesight was gone,
but his mind was still sharp. For hours, he told me about the
things closest to his heart.

Among other things, Dr. Engstrom talked about a pact
that he, Billy Graham, and another close friend, Bill Bright, had
made decades earlier. "We promised each other that we would
finish well," Dr. Engstrom said, smiling winsomely. Then he
added: "And just think—Bill Bright did just that! Billy Graham
assures me he's going to be faithful to the end. And I fully in-
tend to do the same!" Talk about an enduring legacy.

Dr. Engstrom radiated joy. He had made that promise decades earlier, but keeping it wasn't a burden or duty. Instead, it
was the secret of his enthusiasm and vitality. I've seen athletes
flash that same smile after winning a major victory. To see it
radiate from someone near the end of life is even more moving.

Many years ago I made that same promise, and I have
flashed that same smile. I'm happily and fully committed to fin-
ishing well.

---

*Lord, You want courageous men to promise
to be faithful to You until the end. I will tell
others that I have made that promise today.*

TAKE NECESSARY STEPS
TO FINISH WELL

I have fought the good fight, I have
finished the race, I have kept the faith.

2 TIMOTHY 4:7

What will your legacy be? When you get old, will you still have a vital, active faith in Jesus Christ? Sadly, not all do. Dr. J. Robert Clinton has invested much of his career to analyzing why people do—or don't—finish well. He's done a comparative study of more than eight hundred Christian leaders' lives.

His conclusion? "Few leaders finish well." Clinton lists six barriers: (1) finances—their use and abuse, (2) power—its abuse, (3) pride—unchecked, which leads to downfall, (4) sex—illicit relationships, (5) family—unresolved problems, and (6) plateauing—because of sin or loss of vision.

Thankfully, Clinton doesn't stop there. He also lists five reasons why people finish well. All five can be seen in the lives of Bill Bright, Ted Engstrom, Billy Graham, and others: (1) life-time perspective on ministry, (2) fresh encounters with God on occasion, (3) personal disciplines daily, (4) lifelong learning posture, and (5) lifelong mentoring by a number of people.

Lord, You want courageous men to finish well.
You know which barriers I need to overcome.
Help me do what will enable me to finish well.

FACE THE PROBLEM OF "LITTLE" SINS

> You say, "I am allowed to do anything"—but not
> everything is good for you. You say, "I am allowed
> to do anything"—but not everything is beneficial.
>
> 1 CORINTHIANS 10:23 NLT

Most of us don't wake up and say, "I think I'm going to rebel against God and screw up my life today." No, we usually choose to sin by small degrees.

How prone we are to think, *Well, I am forgiven after all, and I'm not quite strong enough to obey that specific command.*

Little sins eventually betray a serious defect deep in our hearts. By "little," of course, I mean little in our eyes, not in God's eyes. Sin is sin. That I'm quite glad not to murder anyone today is no great virtue when I'm just as apt to ignore God's presence in my life.

When we look back at all the little sins we've committed along the way these past few weeks, there may be cause to worry: What's wrong with us? Or, perhaps better put: Why are we so self-inclined and so God-averse? Why are we so apt to choose our will, our way, our timing. . .instead of choosing God's will, God's way, God's timing?

---

*Lord, You want courageous men to choose Your will
over their own. I confess that I have been choosing
my will in the area of _____.*

EMBRACE THE RULES FOR SUCCESSFUL LIVING

Don't you realize that in a race everyone runs,
but only one person gets the prize? So run to win!
All athletes are disciplined in their training. They do
it to win a prize that will fade away, but we do it for
an eternal prize. So I run with purpose in every step.

1 CORINTHIANS 9:24-26 NLT

Many men act as if the rules for successful living are somehow bad. Of course, life's rules are usually good. Take sports, for instance. With clearly defined rules reinforced by the coaches and referees, players can have a lot of fun. Without rules, however, the game quickly turns ugly. It's anything but entertaining, enjoyable, or fun.

The same is true in every sphere of life: sports, education, music, family, church, employment, transportation, technology—you name it. The rules for successful living are important.

Of course, to maintain a higher ideal we sometimes need to break certain rules, which happens every time an ambulance turns on its siren and goes through a red light. We see this in Jesus' own life and ministry. He kept the Ten Commandments perfectly and yet rejected man-made rules that hurt God's people. But always, always, He did God's will in God's way and in God's timing.

Lord, You want courageous men
to do what's best in every circumstance.
Please give me Your wisdom for what I face.

STAY AWAY FROM
MODERN-DAY PHARISEES

"Ignore them [the Pharisees]. They are blind
guides leading the blind, and if one blind person
guides another, they will both fall into a ditch."

MATTHEW 15:14 NLT

We miss God's heart and presence in our lives if we choose to live by rules of our own making. No wonder Jesus repeatedly said that the most important commands are the ones God gives. Sadly, that point was lost on the strictest religious leaders of His day. The Pharisees were out of touch with reality and adamant in their denial of Jesus' person, power, and authority.

The Pharisees had the audacity to demand that Jesus obey their rules. In response, Jesus insisted He was the One who gave the Ten Commandments and inspired the rest of the Old Testament.

To believe Jesus is to believe He is the One who calls the shots. So Jesus told His disciples to stay away from Pharisees. This God-given command applies to us as well. Jesus wants us to stay away from anyone who pretends to speak for God and yet openly and directly opposes what He says.

But how do we achieve this? Go back to God's Word to reread the Gospel accounts of Jesus' life and teachings. Discover God's heart anew. Feel His presence. And fall more in love with the Savior.

---

*Lord, You want courageous men to ignore legalists who
misrepresent You. Please keep me from being legalistic.*

NEVER FORGET SALVATION IS FOREVER

> "For God so loved the world that he gave his
> one and only Son, that whoever believes in
> him shall not perish but have eternal life."
>
> JOHN 3:16

Jesus often talked with His disciples about the evils of this world. His list of evils isn't exhaustive, of course. Jesus could have added other sins that He and Moses and Isaiah and Peter and Paul warned against.

The reality is all the Ten Commandments have been broken by all people in all cultures in all times. Where do these sins come from? Jesus clearly said that they come from inside our hearts (Matthew 15:18–19).

A thousand years earlier, Solomon warned: "Guard your heart" (Proverbs 4:23). If you don't guard your heart, evil things will come out. This applies to every sphere of life. It certainly proved true in Solomon's own experience.

What's more, Jesus' half brother James said that anytime we choose our will over God's revealed will in one specific area, we're actually breaking the whole law of God (James 2:10).

Yes, sin is a temporary reality. Thank God that salvation through Jesus Christ is the eternal solution.

---

*Lord, You want courageous men to
keep an eternal perspective. Thank You
for saving me here and now and forever.*

JESUS WANTS US TO OBEY HIS NEW COMMAND

"Very truly I tell you, no servant is greater than his
master, nor is a messenger greater than the one
who sent him. Now that you know these things,
you will be blessed if you do them."

JOHN 13:16–17

The night before His crucifixion, Jesus wasted no time in communicating what was absolutely foremost on His heart and mind.

To show them the full extent of His love, Jesus washed the disciples' feet. He ate the Passover meal with them and—using the bread and cup—shared the first Christian communion with them. After dismissing Judas the betrayer, Jesus told His disciples one more time that He must die for their sins.

Then He said something startling, revolutionary, and in many ways world changing: "Now I am giving you a new commandment" (John 13:34 NLT).

The disciples must have sat up when Jesus made this proclamation. They'd followed Jesus closely for three and a half years. They'd seen virtually every miracle, heard almost every word of Jesus. Now, with the cross only hours away, the tension rose in the room. They were holding their breath. You can almost feel the sense of anticipation. What was Jesus going to say next?

---

*Lord, You want courageous men to obey Your
commands Your way. Help me understand.*

JESUS CHANGES WHAT IT MEANS TO LOVE

"Your love for one another will prove to
the world that you are my disciples."

JOHN 13:35 NLT

It was the night before His crucifixion. Jesus had washed the disciples' feet. Then He said: "Now I am giving you a new commandment: Love each other" (John 13:34 NLT).

I can imagine Jesus pausing to let the words sink in. Of course, the more they sink in, the more His disciples must have wrinkled their foreheads. *Love each other. That's it?*

I can almost hear Thomas mutter under his breath: "But Jesus, what's new about that? Moses gave us the command to 'Love your neighbor as yourself' about fifteen hundred years ago. You can't get much *older* than that."

Thomas would have had a good point. That is, if Jesus meant only, "Love each other as you love yourselves." But Jesus wasn't finished yet. He went on to say: "Just as I have loved you, you should love each other" (John 13:34 NLT).

In eleven words, Jesus radically changed what it means to love others. It's no longer enough to love them as much as we love ourselves. Jesus calls us to love others as much as *He* loves us.

Lord, You want courageous men to love others as much as Jesus loves them. Help me love _____ today.

THE SECRET OF MONUMENTAL WORLD IMPACT

"Very truly I tell you, whoever believes in me will do the works I have been doing, and they will do even greater things than these, because I am going to the Father."

JOHN 14:12

Everything good that Christianity has done in the past two thousand years has been the fruit of our obedience to Jesus' command to love one another "as I have loved you."

Conversely, everything evil that people have done in the name of Jesus Christ, blaspheming His holy name, has been the fruit of rejecting what Jesus Christ said, especially what He said the night before His crucifixion. I don't care how much such people talk about love. "Love" divorced from God's grace isn't love at all.

But love *with* grace makes all the difference in the world. On your favorite search engine, type "John 13:35" and "William Wilberforce," or "Mother Teresa," or "Billy Graham." You'll find thousands of links. What is the secret of their monumental, positive impact on the world?

May I suggest it isn't a secret at all? They simply knew how to love others as Jesus did: on the basis of Jesus' righteousness, filled with Jesus' grace, year after year, decade after decade—until the whole world *knew* they were Jesus' disciples.

Lord, You want courageous men to do Your works. I will obey You today.

THE FRUIT OF INTIMACY AND SACRIFICE

> "My command is this: Love each other as I have loved you.
> Greater love has no one than this: to lay down one's life for
> one's friends. You are my friends if you do what I command."
> JOHN 15:12-14

The night before dying for our sins, Jesus said these remark-able words: "Your love for one another will prove to the world that you are my disciples" (John 13:35 NLT).

When Jesus used the phrase "your love. . .will prove," he wasn't talking about some kind of intellectual accomplishment. Instead, the Upper Room Discourse, as John 13-17 is often called, shows how the fruit of our love can become a phenom-enal display of the Lord's glory in the world. And what is the fruit of loving as Jesus loved?

The fruit of loving as Jesus loved is obeying Jesus, just as Jesus obeyed His Father to the point of being willing to lay down His life for us. This is the fruit of *sacrifice*.

The fruit of loving as Jesus loved is experiencing unity with God and with each other. This is the fruit of *intimacy*, spiritually and relationally.

The fruit of intimacy and the fruit of sacrifice are insepara-ble. Together, they become an incredible display of the Lord's glory in the world.

---

*Lord, You want courageous men to bear the fruit
of intimacy and sacrifice. Both are hard for me.*

WHAT WE FEEL DOESN'T EQUAL REALITY

Scripture says: "God opposes the proud but shows favor to the humble." Submit yourselves, then, to God. Resist the devil, and he will flee from you. Come near to God and he will come near to you. . . . Humble yourselves before the Lord, and he will lift you up.

JAMES 4:6–8, 10

How often do you have internal arguments with *projections* you have created of other people? Lengthy internal arguments with these mental images can be dangerous. Why? Because they can change our perceptions of the real people, and thus complicate our real-life relationships with them.

It's amazing to watch the lights go on when someone realizes what he feels *doesn't* equal reality. Unfortunately, our culture has made a religion out of equating *consciousness of feelings* with *reality*. Feelings never equate with reality. They're only indicators of how we perceive reality at any given time. And—as it's good to be reminded from time to time—our perceptions never fully approximate reality.

In every situation, my responses to others quickly show my virtue or lack thereof. James 4:10 says: "Humble yourselves before the Lord, and he will lift you up." If we harbor unrelenting anger, we're really denying God. Grace, however, is an encounter with God as He truly is.

Lord, You want courageous men to know reality.
I struggle with negative feelings toward
_____. Change my heart, I pray.

GRIPPED BY THE LORD'S AMAZING, SACRIFICIAL LOVE

*For it seems to me that God has put us apostles
on display at the end of the procession,
like those condemned to die in the arena.*

1 CORINTHIANS 4:9

It's one thing to know that on the night before His crucifixion, Jesus said these remarkable words: "Your love for one another will prove to the world that you are my disciples" (John 13:35 NLT). But do we have any evidence that the disciples took this to heart?

Thankfully, the answer is a resounding yes!

We find similar injunctions in the writings of the apostles Peter, James, John, and Paul. In fact, John and Paul couldn't stop talking about it.

More importantly, each of the apostles, to his dying day, was renowned for his intimate walk with God, his passion for unity within the Church, and his sacrificial love. To a man, they were willing to die a martyr's death, following the example of their Lord and Savior. They took the Gospel of Jesus Christ west from Antioch to Spain and east from Jerusalem to India.

What compelled them to give their lives fully in the Lord's service? The amazing, intimate, sacrificial love that God the Father and Jesus demonstrated to us and the rest of the world. What love, indeed!

---

*Lord, You want courageous men to obey and follow
Jesus until the day they die. I want to be such a man.*

THE LORD'S AMAZING LOVE MOTIVATES US

*Dear friends, let us continue to love
one another, for love comes from God.*

1 JOHN 4:7 NLT

My attention often is drawn back to the amazing love of God the Father and Jesus. The apostle John experienced this too. In the first of his three epistles, John wrote: "Anyone who loves is a child of God and knows God. But anyone who does not love does not know God, for God is love" (1 John 4:7–8 NLT).

But John couldn't stop there, so he kept writing: "God showed how much he loved us by sending his one and only Son into the world so that we might have eternal life through him. This is real love—not that we loved God, but that he loved us and sent his Son as a sacrifice to take away our sins" (verses 9–10 NLT).

Still, John couldn't stop, so he added: "Dear friends, since God loved us that much, we surely ought to love each other. No one has ever seen God. But if we love each other, God lives in us, and his love is brought to full expression in us" (verses 11–12 NLT).

John continued to write about this amazing love for three more paragraphs in 1 John 4 alone, plus in dozens of other passages. What love, indeed!

---

*Lord, You want courageous men to love You and others
without fail. I struggle with this. Change my heart.*

THE LORD'S AMAZING LOVE
MAKES A DIFFERENCE!

Your love has given me great joy and encouragement,
because you, brother, have refreshed the hearts of the
Lord's people. Therefore, although in Christ I could
be bold and order you to do what you ought to do,
yet I prefer to appeal to you on the basis of love.

PHILEMON 7–9

As you read the New Testament letters of Paul, you soon discover that he couldn't stop writing about the amazing, intimate, sacrificial love of God the Father and Jesus His Son. He never stopped marveling that God demonstrated the full extent of His love by giving His Son, who in turn gave His life for us.

It was to this high standard of love—Jesus' own love—that the aged apostle appealed when he wrote to his dear friend Philemon. That short letter is a majestic example of persuasive writing. In it, Paul urged Philemon to spare the life of his runaway slave, Onesimus, and instead embrace him as a new brother in Jesus Christ.

So, did Jesus' new commandment—to love as He loved—make any significant, observable, and ultimately meaningful difference in Paul's life? Yes!

It can do the same in our lives too.

Lord, You want courageous men to love like Jesus even at
great personal cost. How do You want me to do that?

THE LORD'S AMAZING LOVE IN ACTION

"Love your enemies, do good to them, and lend to them
without expecting to get anything back. Then your reward
will be great, and you will be children of the Most High,
because he is kind to the ungrateful and wicked."

LUKE 6:35

Think of the energy exerted by the crowd at a sold-out concert
or an exciting sporting event. Now think of the even greater
amount of energy exerted by someone who serves God and
others faithfully year after year, decade after decade.

When you think how much God loves us, how much energy
are you willing to exert loving other people? How intimate are
you willing to be? How much are you willing to sacrifice?

More specifically, who are you choosing to love? Does anyone come to mind? Who is he? Say his name in your mind. Say,
"Yes, Lord, I'm choosing to love him." It may mean getting to
know him better. It may mean sacrificing something. Who are
you choosing to love?

Perhaps you're thinking of someone whose health is poor
or who serves others quietly without fanfare. Maybe it's a
family member or someone you have a hard time getting along
with. Again, who are you choosing to love?

_____

Lord, You want courageous men to love others daily.
Help me show Your love to _____ *today.*

WHO IS IN GOD'S KINGDOM? PART 1

> "I issue a decree that in every part of my kingdom people
> must fear and reverence the God of Daniel. For he is
> the living God and he endures forever; his kingdom will
> not be destroyed, his dominion will never end."
>
> DANIEL 6:26

As we read scripture, we come across a number of compelling questions. One of these questions is, "Who is in God's kingdom?"

Daniel 6:25–27 addresses this question. Read the verses carefully: "Then King Darius wrote to all the nations and peoples of every language in all the earth: 'May you prosper greatly! I issue a decree that in every part of my kingdom people must fear and reverence the God of Daniel. For he is the living God and he endures forever; his kingdom will not be destroyed, his dominion will never end. He rescues and he saves; he performs signs and wonders in the heavens and on the earth. He has rescued Daniel from the power of the lions.' "

Let's not forget who said these words. This was King Darius, ruler of the known world. His armies toppled the Babylonian empire. Yet here he was speaking about God's kingdom. And he told everyone in every part of his kingdom to fear and reverence the God of Daniel.

So, who is part of God's kingdom? Scripture surprises us by answering: everyone.

---

*Lord, You want courageous men to serve in
Your kingdom forever. Here am I, Your servant.*

WHO IS IN GOD'S KINGDOM? PART 2

For he has rescued us from the dominion of darkness
and brought us into the kingdom of the Son he loves,
in whom we have redemption, the forgiveness of sins.

COLOSSIANS 1:13–14

In Daniel 2–6 we find pagan kings making amazing declarations. They repeatedly state what you and I already know: that God's kingdom and rule extends over everything in heaven and earth—not just emperors and kings, but over all people in all the earth.

The implication is rather startling yet obvious. Every human being on earth is a servant of God Most High. They are servants no matter how high or low, rich or poor, powerful or weak, proud or humble.

So that it's crystal clear: only redeemed believers and followers of Jesus Christ are "citizens" of God's kingdom, but all human beings everywhere are "servants" in God's kingdom.

Whatever you're doing to serve others, keep doing it. But this week, switch things 180 degrees. Think about ways your neighbors can serve you. After all, everybody around you is a servant in God's kingdom. And their service to you can open a beautiful door to their coming salvation.

---

*Lord, You want courageous men to invite
servants in Your kingdom to serve them. I plan to
ask _____ to serve me this coming weekend.*

WHO IS IN GOD'S KINGDOM? PART 3

For you know that we dealt with each of you as
a father deals with his own children, encouraging,
comforting and urging you to live lives worthy of
God, who calls you into his kingdom and glory.

1 THESSALONIANS 2:11-12

Scripture tells us many things about God's kingdom.

First, without question, Jesus Christ is the rightful, exalted King of God's kingdom.

Second, God's kingdom is the context through which He is advancing His purposes here on earth.

Third, that context includes God's work through kings, prime ministers, presidents, governors, mayors, and other government officials, whether or not they believe in God. If God could use ancient pharaohs, mighty emperors, and Roman Caesars, believe me, God can use anyone. And He will do so right up until the end of time.

We see this in Revelation 21:24: "The nations will walk by [God's] light, and the kings of the earth will bring their splendor into it." Two verses later, in Revelation 21:26, we read: "The glory and honor of the nations will be brought into" the eternal city of God.

I'm so thankful that God can use anyone to advance His purposes here on earth. And He continues to advance His purposes undeterred by who is or isn't in power around the globe. So, be encouraged!

Lord, You want courageous men to trust You as they keep the faith here on earth. I reaffirm my trust in You and Your glory.

WHO IS IN GOD'S KINGDOM? PART 4

The Lord will rescue me from every evil attack
and will bring me safely to his heavenly kingdom.
To him be glory for ever and ever. Amen.

2 TIMOTHY 4:18

I've been asked, "What's the take-away value of looking at God's kingdom in light of eternity?"

I find it puts a whole new perspective on everything in this life. It reminds me that it doesn't matter what happens in China, Russia, the Middle East, and the United States. It doesn't matter how bad or good things get on Wall Street. It doesn't matter who is in the White House. No matter what, God's kingdom is advancing His purposes through humanity here on earth.

It grieves me when we look at someone who is different from us, economically or politically or socially, and assume that God can't use that individual. God can use anyone to advance His purposes, and what's more, He often uses them as a means of drawing them into His family and church today.

Remember, not all "servants" in God's kingdom are "citizens" yet. Citizens are going to spend eternity with God. Servants may or may not. God's desire, of course, is that none perish but that all come to repentance (2 Peter 3:9). That should be our desire as well. Amen?

Lord, You want courageous men to invite
servants to become citizens of Your kingdom.
I will spend more time with _____.

WHO IS MY NEIGHBOR?

Each of us should please our neighbors
for their good, to build them up.

ROMANS 15:2

Another intriguing question we come across in the Bible is, "Who is my neighbor?"

The scripture that *raises* this question is the Great Commandment taught by Jesus in Matthew 22:34–40 and in Mark 12:28–34. The second half of the Great Commandment says, "Love your neighbor as yourself." Of course, that begs the question, "Who is my neighbor?"

People in Jesus' day wanted to know what the right answer was. People around the world today—whether Jewish, Christian, or whatever—want to know the right answer as well. The question "Who is my neighbor?" is too compelling to leave unanswered.

Thankfully, the scripture that *answers* this question is one of Jesus' most famous stories—the parable of the good Samaritan found in Luke 10:25–37. You might know the story well, but take a few minutes now to read through the text. . . .

The answer Jesus gives is clear-cut. Everyone around me is my neighbor. That's why I believe it's so important to give tithes and offerings to my local church and the ministries it supports. I encourage you to do the same.

---

*Lord, You want courageous men to love their neighbors—
and that includes everyone in my community and
beyond. I commit to giving generously.*

WHO IS MY BROTHER? PART 1

"And the King will answer them, 'Truly, I say
to you, as you did it to one of the least of
these my brothers, you did it to me.'"

MATTHEW 25:40 ESV

One more compelling question from scripture is, "Who is my brother?"

In Matthew 25, Jesus talked about the end of time when He divides the sheep from the goats. The sheep, of course, are those who know and believe and follow Jesus Christ.

In His account, the Lord thanks the sheep for all they did for Him. These believers from all around the world and down through the ages, all the way back to Adam and Eve, are stymied. "When did we do all that?" they ask. Jesus' reply is recorded in Matthew 25:40 and gives us our answer to "Who is my brother?" "The least of these"—the poorest of the poor, the homeless, prisoners, the downtrodden, the oppressed—Jesus calls "my brothers."

When we talk with people who aren't Christians yet and call them our "brother," we're not pretending that they have trusted Jesus Christ. (But don't be surprised if they do come to Christ!) Therefore, if the Lord moves you to call someone "brother," don't hesitate. Follow the Lord's own example. Say "brother" as a way of reinforcing our common bond with our neighbors.

Lord, You want courageous men to expand their vision of
"brother." Please help me see everyone as my brother.

WHO IS MY BROTHER?
PART 2

Then he looked at those seated in a circle around him
and said, "Here are my mother and my brothers!"

MARK 3:34

In sixteen passages in Matthew, Mark, Luke, and John, Jesus redefined "brothers" to refer not just to His apostles, not just to His followers, and not just to our relationship with each other, but also to our relationship with all other people.

The implication is clear and startling: we should say "brother" whenever we speak to and about other Christians *and* we should call everyone else "brother" too.

When you and I call each other "brother," we're usually speaking about our special bond as brothers in Christ. That's important. Let's never stop that.

Yet in Matthew 25:40 and other passages, Jesus went much further. When we talk with people who aren't Christians yet and call them our "brother" or "sister," we're reinforcing our common bond and relationship as neighbors.

In other words, the question isn't just "Who is my neighbor?" but also "Who is my brother?" And Jesus' answer to both questions is the same: it's everyone we know and meet.

Lord, You want courageous men to call all other men "brothers." I will call _____ my brother.

WHO IS MY BROTHER?
PART 3

To this he replied: "Brothers and fathers, listen to me!
The God of glory appeared to our father Abraham while
he was still in Mesopotamia, before he lived in Harran."

ACTS 7:2

"Who is my brother?" In the Gospels, Jesus said to think of all people as our brothers.

When we turn from the four Gospels to the book of Acts, we see the early Church doing just that.

In a total of twenty-six passages from Acts 1 to Acts 28, "brothers" is used as a general term to speak about any group of people with whom believers shared some sort of common ground—whether racial, regional, religious, or otherwise. This is rather remarkable. Peter, Stephen, Paul, and other early Church leaders didn't just use the term "brothers" when talking with other followers of Jesus Christ. They also used the term "brothers" with everyone else.

Likewise, as the Lord moves us, we should say "brothers" when we speak with people from all kinds of backgrounds. We should use the term "brothers" as a means to reinforce our common ground—and to gain instant rapport.

If the Lord nudges you to call someone "brother" or "sister," don't allow doubts to hold you back. Follow the example of Jesus and the early Church—with confidence.

*Lord, You want courageous men to speak about their
"brothers" often. Help me overcome my reluctance.*

WHO IS MY BROTHER?
PART 4

"Brothers and fathers, listen now to my defense."

ACTS 22:1

"Who is my brother?" On multiple occasions, Stephen and Paul took things to an unexpected level.

We see this first in Acts 7 right before Stephen is martyred. The first word out of his mouth when he faced his enemies was *brothers* (Acts 7:2). When I first read this, I was shocked. Was that a slipup? But it becomes a pattern.

When Paul faced possible martyrdom, the first word out of his mouth in Acts 22 isn't *enemies*. No, instead, it's *brothers* (Acts 22:1). Ditto in the very next chapter. Not *enemies*, though they were that, to be sure. But Paul again referred to them as his brothers (Acts 23:1).

Thankfully, we don't have the same kinds of enemies with the power and passion to make us martyrs. Still, what Stephen and Paul did takes the definition of "Who is my brother?" to the *n*th degree.

Bottom line: you and I *never* have to hesitate and wonder whether we can call someone our brother. Instead, follow the examples of Stephen and Paul. Heed the Lord's own example in the Gospels. Say the word *brother*.

Lord, You want courageous men to
call their enemies "brothers." I will
call _____ my brother.

WHO IS IN GOD'S FAMILY?

Both the one who makes people holy and those
who are made holy are of the same family. So Jesus
is not ashamed to call them brothers and sisters.

HEBREWS 2:11

One more compelling question we come across in scripture is, "Who is in God's family?"

God's family stretches from Adam and Eve to today and beyond.

First, God's family includes all authentic followers of Jesus Christ who belong to the Church.

Second, God's family includes all authentic Jewish believers in Old Testament times.

Third, God's family includes even more ancient individuals like Noah, Job, and Abraham, who believed in God long before the ancient Israelite nation, the Jewish faith, and the Hebrew scriptures existed. Among other places, we see this in Revelation 22:16, where Jesus said, "I am the Root and the Offspring of David, and the bright Morning Star." There He spoke both to the ancient Jewish people who believed in Him and to others who, like the ancient magi, saw God's reality, power, beauty, and might in creation and passionately longed for that reality in their own lives. Those who seek God will always find Him.

I'm so very thankful that we can be sure eternity will be enjoyed by all of God's family down through the ages.

---

*Lord, You want courageous men to embrace a larger
vision of Your family. I believe it includes all believers
from Adam and Eve to today and beyond.*

EATING WITH OTHERS LIKE JESUS

As Jesus went on from there, he saw a man named Matthew
sitting at the tax collector's booth. "Follow me," he told him,
and Matthew got up and followed him.

MATTHEW 9:9

Do you like going to fancy dinners, banquets, and feasts? Jesus
did! He enjoyed the opportunity to meet new people and whet
their appetite for the kingdom of God.

When Jesus invited Matthew to become one of His disciples, Matthew must have been shocked. Yet immediately
he gave up his lucrative tax-collecting business and held
a huge banquet that evening. The banquet wasn't in Matthew's
honor—a "retirement" party of sorts. Instead, Matthew somehow knew that Jesus wanted to meet his friends. So he invited
them over to his home.

Sure enough, the word about Matthew's party got out to
that city's religious elite, who condemned Jesus. Jesus used
their harsh criticisms, however, as an opportunity to demonstrate His love and compassion for the "scum" of the earth.

Like Matthew, you have work associates, friends, neighbors, and relatives who don't know the Lord yet. Some may be
rather shady characters. But the Lord loves them and wants
you to eat with them and find a way to introduce them to the
Savior.

---

*Lord, You want courageous men to practice generous
hospitality with one and all. Please show me who
I should invite over for dinner this week.*

GOD CARES FOR EVERYONE, PART 1

You evildoers frustrate the plans of
the poor, but the LORD is their refuge.

PSALM 14:6

I'm so thankful God cares for every person we know and meet. The Bible clearly teaches that "everyone" includes the fatherless and widows, the afflicted and suffering, the helpless and hungry, the lonely and brokenhearted, the blind and broken, the prisoner and oppressed.

In particular, I'm thankful for these five divine truths.

1. The Lord loves the poor and needy. He makes them the object of His love, protection, and concern (Deuteronomy 15:11).

2. Scripture repeatedly says that God hears their cries. More than that, the Lord defends them and encourages them (Psalm 10:17–18). He is their sure refuge (Psalm 14:6).

3. The Lord delivers the needy from the oppression of the wicked (Psalm 35:10).

4. The Bible makes it crystal clear that God doesn't despise or disdain the destitute (Psalm 22:24). Instead, the Lord gladly provides their daily bread (Psalm 68:10).

5. God makes their hearts alive again with joy (Psalm 69:32) and answers their heartfelt prayers (Psalm 102:17).

No wonder we're to cast our cares on the Lord, for He cares for us (1 Peter 5:7).

---

*Lord, You want courageous men to cast their
cares on You. Thank You for caring for me.*

GOD CARES FOR EVERYONE, PART 2

People who boast of their wealth don't
understand; they will die, just like animals.

PSALM 49:20 NLT

I'm so thankful the Lord cares for us. He also cares for the homeless, helpless, and hopeless. This is true whether their own parents forsake them (Psalm 27:10) or they have been afflicted for one reason or another since their youth (Psalm 88:15). This is also true if a close friend turns against them (Psalm 55:12–14), which happened to King David and, centuries later, to Jesus when He was betrayed.

Again, I'm so thankful the Lord cares for everyone. Often, however, God's rich blessings go unclaimed because people refuse to listen to Him or follow His ways (Psalm 81:11–16). This has been true since days of old (Psalm 78:7–8). Still, God stands ever ready to bless people if they turn to Him in repentance (Psalm 106:4–6), no matter what their current situation (Psalm 107).

What's more, I'm so glad David declared this divine truth: riches without a right relationship with God are worthless (Psalm 49:20).

---

*Lord, You want courageous men to trust Your
care for them here and now and for eternity.
I never need fear Your lack of care for me.*

ARE YOU GROWING STRONG?

Be strong and immovable. Always work
enthusiastically for the Lord, for you know that
nothing you do for the Lord is ever useless.

1 CORINTHIANS 15:58 NLT

Someone much older and wiser than me—B. F. Westcott—once
said, "Silently and imperceptibly as we work or sleep, we grow
strong or we grow weak; and at least some crisis shows us what
we have become." He added that crises "do not make heroes or
cowards; they simply reveal them."

So, what kind of man are you becoming? Are you becoming a man of backbone, boldness, determination, durability,
faithfulness, fortitude, grit, guts, mettle, moxie, patience, persistence, resilience, resolution, stamina, staying power, steadfastness, straightforwardness, stick-to-it-iveness, tenacity, and
toughness?

What's more, do you know the meaning of adversity, bravery, conviction, discipline, endurance, fearlessness, gratitude,
hardship, insult, joy, keeping the faith, listening to the Lord,
motivation, never giving up, oppression, perseverance, quietness, righteousness, strength, trustworthiness, understanding,
vibrancy, wholeheartedness, expectation, yearning, and zeal for
the Lord?

---

*Lord, You want men to become more and more
courageous. As time goes on, I want to grow strong.*

CHOOSE COURAGE WITH OTHERS

What you have heard from me in the presence
of many witnesses entrust to faithful men,
who will be able to teach others also.

2 TIMOTHY 2:2 ESV

You're almost done reading this book, but whatever you do, don't put it away on some shelf. Instead, I highly recommend that you read it again. This second time through, highlight truths you want to remember for years to come.

After that, still don't put this book on a shelf. Instead, sign and date the inside front cover. Then show this book to a friend. Let him see how you've signed and dated this book after reading it twice. Let him flip through the pages for a minute or two or three. Find out if he would like to read a new copy you just happen to have on hand. Assure him that "Yes" is a great answer and "No" is a great answer as well.

Whether your friend says yes or no, still don't put this book away. Instead, keep using it as show-and-tell with another friend here, a third friend there—until you have a team of five or more friends reading *Choose Courage*.

The reward? You'll grow strong and so will they. In fact, your friends will thank you for inspiring them. Some might thank you repeatedly. Each time, simply smile and give God the glory.

SCRIPTURE INDEX

MORE GREAT DEVOTIONS FOR MEN

Guys, here are devotional readings based on one hundred key Bible words and concepts—including Authority, Calm, Focus, Perseverance, and Victory. You'll be inspired to think deeply on God and His Word, "which is able to make you wise for salvation through faith which is in Christ Jesus" (2 Timothy 3:15 NKJV).

Hardcover / 978-1-64352-219-7 / $12.99